Home Run

The Personal Profiles of Champion Athletes

By Paul Knowles

Forward by Gary Carter

Mainroads Productions Inc.
100 Huntley Street
Toronto, Ontario
M4Y 2L1

Copyright 1986 © MAINROADS PRODUCTIONS INC.

1st PRINTING – 1986
2nd PRINTING – 1986

ISBN 0-919463-13-4

Published by MAINROADS PRODUCTIONS INC.
100 Huntley Street, Toronto, Ontario M4Y 2L1

Printed in Canada
Harmony Printing Limited
123 Eastside Drive, Toronto, Ontario M8Z 5S5

Photo Credits: Toronto Blue Jays
                 David Helsdon
                 Pam Mark
                 Paul Knowles

Front Cover: The Redeemer...Lloyd Moseby, whose error cost the Jays' a 4-3 loss to New York a game earlier, smacked a homer which led the club to a title-clinching win for the 1985 American League East Championship. (Canada Wide — Stan Behl)

Dedication

For Luke and Aaron –

*You may never play ball like Jesse or Lloyd,
but may you learn to live like them.*

Contents

Foreword

By Gary Carter
All-Star catcher of the New York Mets

I am pleased to be asked to contribute the foreword to this book about a group of fine baseball players.

From my years with the Montreal Expos, I have a real love for Canadian baseball, and a deep appreciation of the Canadian baseball fans. I know, that in Montreal, in Toronto and in cities and towns from coast to coast in Canada, baseball is alive and well.

I want to congratulate Jesse Barfield, Lloyd Moseby, Willie Upshaw, Tony Fernandez and the rest of the Toronto Blue Jays for their great season in 1985, and I wish them all the best as they strive for continued excellence. I admire the team, and I respect the ballplayers whose stories are told in this book. These are men of excellence, on and off the diamond – fine athletes, and men of courage and integrity.

Their baseball skills are to be admired, and their lives are good examples of the positive things that can be accomplished by professional athletes. They have discovered some keys to successful living that I, too, have found; they have the peace and happiness that can be elusive in the high-pressure world of major league sport.

I commend Paul Knowles for writing *Home Run*, telling the behind-the-scenes stories of men who are on the sports pages every day. I gladly recommend this book to Blue Jays' fans, baseball fans, sports fans in general and anyone else who likes a good story.

Chapter 1

"Let's Play Ball"

"O.K., Blue Jays, *let's play ball!*"

The cry has echoed across the artificial turf at Exhibition Stadium on Toronto's waterfront for 10 years, but never with more emotional intensity than during the summer months of 1985. The Toronto Blue Jays had come of age – their pitchers were pitching, their hitters were hitting, and every game seemed to provide an array of electrifying plays that brought the traditionally staid southern Ontario fans screaming off their chairs and benches.

By the end of the season, the Blue Jays had won the American League East championship and, as Maclean's magazine said, had eclipsed the Montreal Expos as "Canada's team."

It didn't seem to matter that "Canada's team" was playing the quintessential American game; that the team had no Canadians on the field (not since third baseman Dave McKay left in its infancy); that most of the players spoke with a distinctly American accent or struggled with English, a language seldom heard in their native Dominican Republic.

9

It didn't matter at all. These were our Blue Jays, and they were winners! And they were more than just the *Toronto* Blue Jays; despite the name, these were clearly Canada Jays, loved country-wide. Some would say the Blue Jays are the only thing other Canadians love about Toronto.

But the issue was never politics (although we do love to beat the Yankees, both as a team and as a nation) or regionalism. The crack of the bat and the 'smack' of the ball hitting a glove sparked that simple love of sport in millions of fans who are well past their last home run or stolen base. Every Canadian child who's held a hockey stick in the winter has also played T-ball, slow-pitch, scrub, softball or baseball in spring and summer. We all know the wonderful feeling of smacking a single between second and first or of stretching for that line drive and finding the ball, miraculously, in our gloves.

A lot of us also know the feeling of being chosen last for the team and finding ourselves stuck out in right field – the unkindest cut of all in schoolyard baseball. But wait – out in right field for the Toronto Blue Jays is the guy voted Most Valuable Player on the whole team, Jesse Barfield. Each time Barfield blasted a home run, ran down an impossible fly or gunned out a runner at home plate, every insulted right-fielder in the land stood up and cheered.

To a city saddled with an up and down sports tradition (usually more downs than ups), the Toronto Blue Jays were an affirmation. Toronto is a winner after all. To all of us who live beyond the boundaries of Metro, the Blue Jays weren't from Toronto at all. Maclean's was right; they're Canada's team.

In recent seasons, drug scandals have folded, spindled and multilated major league baseball.

Canada's team stayed clear of any such problems. Probably the strongest drug in the locker room was the caffeine in pre-batting practice coffee. While the American teams tried to wipe the cocaine-scented grime from their uniforms, the Jays just played great baseball.

New heroes emerged in 1985 to join those already revered, such as Dave Steib and Ernie Whitt. Fans thrilled to the acrobatic antics of Tony Fernandez, the lithe and whip-quick shortstop who proved that the Blue Jays were right in trading perennial favourite Alfredo Griffin to make room for his young Dominican compatriot. Fernandez's patented side-arm flick to first has undoubtedly influenced thousands of aspiring shortstops patrolling the gap on little league fields.

When the opposition had a man on second, Toronto fans practically prayed for a single into right, just for a chance to see another phenomenal bullet to home plate from the awesome arm of Jesse Barfield. Thousands stood and cheered when Jesse's friend Lloyd Moseby atoned for a breath-snatching error in the final series against the Yankees by smashing a home run the very next night.

The highlights go on and on, and every fan has a favourite memory. The list of stars includes the whole Blue Jay line-up, and every fan has his or her own special Jay.

Toronto's Boys of Summer are now in the early stages of the 1986 season. Expectations are even higher, though most knowledgeable baseball folk admit the Jays are in the toughest of divisions, up against the likes of the Detroit Tigers, the New York Yankees, the Boston Red Sox and the Baltimore Orioles, teams of talent and tradition.

But the Blue Jays clearly have the talent to build

their own tradition. And a team history that was once the story of brave underdogs, losing yet again, is now the saga of the champions. Blue Jay brass won't predict another championship – they don't want to saddle their ballplayers with such an expectation. But everyone in the head office is of one mind with the fans – the Eastern championship was wonderful, but this year the Jays want the American League pennant, and the World Series rings.

That may not happen. The intricacies of baseball mitigate against effective prediction. Most American sportswriters are picking either the Tigers or the Yankees in the AL East in 1986. But Blue Jays fans think they know better – and the Blue Jay players very much want to prove their supporters right.

A couple of things are guaranteed. First, the well over two million Jays fans who will attend games (not to speak of millions more television watchers or those who've made baseball radio broadcasts a regular feature of warm Canadian summer afternoons) will experience some great baseball in 1986. The core of a wonderful team is back untouched, and improved by a year of big league experience. The bench strength is probably better than in 1985, with the addition of such Jays as Kelly Gruber. And young pitchers – Steve Davis . . . Mark Eichhorn – have bolstered the remarkable Blue Jay pitching staff.

This isn't a book of predictions for 1986. And it isn't a book that describes the great game of baseball. No prose conveys the pleasure of sitting in the stands at Exhibition Stadium wearing a Blue Jays cap, munching a hot dog and dumping your Coke over the back of the guy in front of you when you stand to cheer a Willie Upshaw home run.

Rather, this is a book about some of the men who carried us with their gloves and bats to the euphoria of the American League championship series last year. This is a book about members of the team who will be giving everything they have to go even farther on the bases this year – all the way to the World Series.

This is a book about great baseball players who are also fine men – thoughtful, intense, humourous men who know that life goes on off the diamond and who are living life the way they play ball – with honour, energy and purpose.

In these pages you'll meet slugging right fielder Jesse Barfield and discover that, despite his MVP status, there are other, even more important elements in his life. You'll hear great centre fielder Lloyd Moseby talk about how he copes with success and failure – and who it is who actually steals Willie Upshaw's game glove.

You'll meet solid first baseman Willie Upshaw and be granted a glimpse behind this man's shy exterior. You'll read about the early years of Tony Fernandez and discover what drove him to succeed in the major leagues – and the different reality that directs him now. You'll also come to know relief pitcher Gary Lavelle, who moved to the Jays after a long career with the San Francisco Giants, and you'll discover the bond that grew between this veteran white pitcher and a group of young black superstars.

You'll also be introduced to some of the fledgling Jays – young baseball players who are just starting in the big leagues. One is Kelly Gruber, who earned his way into a Jays uniform in spring training by playing seven different positions on the team and

13

consistently hitting long balls. Steve Davis, the left-hander, hurled his way into the bullpen; Steve's friend, Don Gordon, played so well in Florida this spring that the Blue Jay office found an unexpected place for him on the club; and Mark Eichhorn came into camp as a non-roster player, but earned the right to start this season as the Jays' tenth pitcher.

In these pages you'll also read some less-than-success stories. Two of them concern men who spent time with the Jays last season but started this year with the minor-league Syracuse Chiefs: catcher Jeff Hearron, who has returned to the Jays since an injury sidelined catcher Ernie Whitt, and outfielder Ron Shepherd, also called up in mid-season. You'll discover how they cope with the disappointments that can send a player back to the minors.

You've cheered for these men and chanted their names on summer afternoons and evenings lit by banks of lights. I know that, as you meet them, from Barfield to Gordon, you're going to like them even more. They're great ballplayers, but they're also very fine people. I hope that you discover something of what makes them tick, what they're like off the field, as you hear their stories in their own unique voices.

I'm deeply indebted to each one of these Blue Jays for their enthusiastic cooperation in preparing this book. I hope they enjoy it half as much as I enjoyed getting to know them. Thanks, also, to several people who went well out of their way to assist me in this project: Blue Jays' chaplain David Fisher, broadcaster Jerry Haworth and Blue Jays' public relations director Howard Starkman.

O.K., Blue Jays, lets play ball.

Chapter 2

Jesse Barfield

"It's a long single into right field. The runner from second is rounding third and heading for home. Barfield is up with the ball . . . he throws a rocket to catcher Ernie Whitt . . . the runner is out!"

That drama was enacted time and again in 1985 at Exhibition Stadium and in ball parks around the American League cities. Many knowledgeable baseball people contend that Jesse Barfield, Blue Jay number 29, has the best arm of any fielder in the game today.

Last year, Barfield's arm, in potent combination with fielding that probably should have earned him a Gold Glove, and a career-high batting average of .289 and 27 home runs, earned him honours as Toronto Blue Jays' Most Valuable Player. New Blue Jays' manager Jimy Williams admits he is understating the case when he says, "He had a good season in 1985, to say the least."

Jesse sees the MVP award as an acknowledgement of his leadership on the Jays. He says, "That was one of my goals, to be a team leader. I think I led by example more than anything last year. I was thrilled!"

15

Where do you go from being Most Valuable Player? Blue Jays' batting coach Cito Gaston believes Jesse Barfield is still on the way up. He insists, "I'll tell you what, Jesse can do a lot of things for you. He can play the outfield, he has a great arm, he can steal some bases, hit with power. We've yet to really get the full talent out of Jesse, as far as I'm concerned. I think Jesse could probably hit more home runs, and his average has been going up every year. He's got a chance to be a superstar."

That's about as crisp and direct an assessment as you're going to get anywhere!

Both Jesse and the Jays are celebrating their 10th anniversary in baseball in 1986. In 1977, the year the Blue Jays first took the field, Jesse Barfield began his professional baseball career in "A" ball at Utica, New York. He had been chosen well down in the pack in the 1977 Free Agent Draft. The Jays selected Barfield in the ninth round – the two hundred and thirty-third choice overall that year. Jesse isn't the first successful ballplayer to be chosen after hundreds of other prospects, but that kind of initiation can't be the most confidence-building of experiences.

And to shake his confidence further, the eighteen-year-old right fielder slumped badly in his second season, played in Dunedin, Florida, where he hit only .206, and managed only two home runs in 133 games.

But when Jesse gets a bead on a fly ball, the odds are good that it will find his glove. Barfield had a bead on the major leagues and came back from his terrible 1978 season to put together his best minor league campaign ever, playing "A" ball in Kinston in the Carolina league.

16

It took two more years to make the big club in Toronto, but the Jays rewarded his good Kinston year by promoting Jesse to the club's 40-man major league roster in October 1979. After spring training each year Jesse was sent to the Knoxville Tennessee "AA" division club to get his bats and experience. But in September 1981 the call came that every minor league player anxiously awaits: there was a Blue Jays uniform with his name on it. Jesse joined the club with a game in Chicago and contributed one hit, a run batted in, and a stolen base in that first game.

He hasn't put on a minor league uniform since.

After coming to the major league club, Barfield has simply got better and better. He is one-third of the trio usually called "the best young outfield in the major leagues" – Barfield in right field, Lloyd Moseby in centre, and George Bell in left. Recently the word "young" more often is dropped from that assessment, and the three are simply included among the best . . . period. The Toronto Sun called the trio "one of the strongest in baseball, maybe the best all-around." But they're still young – all three were born within a month of one another in 1959. Jesse Barfield turns 27 on October 29, 1986; Bell on October 21; Moseby on November 5.

Barfield's batting average has increased consistently year by year – from .232 in that first partial campaign to .284 in 1984, and in his best hitting yet, .289 in 1985. For that season Jesse wasn't "platooned" – he had previously shared his position with a left-handed batter who would hit against right-handed pitchers, while right-handed Barfield would hit against lefties. But the Jays knew they had to make more room for the obviously

17

talented right fielder and traded Dave Collins to provide a permanent spot to the right of Lloyd Moseby. Barfield responded with his best average ever as he took on both left- and right-handed pitchers.

The 1985 season saw a lot of personal bests for Jesse Barfield. He hit safely in 10 of the Jays' first 11 games. He tore up opposing pitchers on a 16-game streak with at least one hit every game, including seven home runs and 13 runs batted in during that period. He tied a club record by swatting homers in three consecutive games, against Minnesota and Chicago. And he reached base safely in 24 consecutive games. In the field, Barfield set a club record with 22 outfield assists. In other words, the gun he calls his right arm picked off 22 opposing players on the base paths.

These figures culminated in his being named Blue Jays' Most Valuable Player.

Jesse Barfield's love for baseball goes way back. He grew up in Joliet, Illinois near Chicago, and spent a lot of hours in the bleachers of Wrigley Field watching the Chicago Cubs. He set his sights on big league ball when he was 12 years old, inspired by the players he cheered week after week.

Jesse recalls, "I used to watch Ernie Banks and Billy Williams and all those guys at Wrigley Field." And if there wasn't a game at Wrigley, Jesse would skip across town to watch the White Sox. He admits that it wasn't long before "I wanted to be out there with them." Jesse's prospects began to take shape while attending Joliet Central High School, where his skills shone brightly. Barfield was named to the All-Conference team and the All-American First Team.

The Barfield home in Joliet had known family separation and sorrow. Jesse says, "My Mom raised us. My Dad and Mom separated when I was real young, and she did a tremendous job. I owe her a lot."

But even though Mrs. Barfield gave everything she could to her family, there is no doubt that Jesse felt the pain of an absent father and a broken home. And yet, soon after he became a full-time member of the Toronto Blue Jays, Jesse's marriage to his petite wife, Marla, was heading in that same direction.

Jesse remembers those days with pain in his voice: "I was struggling, and not just on the field. I'd have to say that the biggest part of my problem was off the field. I wasn't happy with myself. I had no joy at all." His frustration with life threatened their young marriage. And he knew that no success on the baseball diamond would keep the wedding ring on his wife's hand.

Yet today, Jesse and Marla, usually seen with young Joshua and Jessica, are radiantly happy. Jesse himself says, "I have a great family relationship now. My wife and I understand each other."

Marla Barfield remembers the night that everything turned around: "I'll never forget that date. It was June 28, 1982." And another Blue Jay, Roy Lee Jackson, was a main character in the event.

If the eleven ballplayers whose stories make up this book ever vote for a Blue Jay "Most Valuable Player," he just might be a man who had an up-and-down career as a relief pitcher – Roy Lee Jackson. Jackson was cut from the Jays during spring training in 1985. Picked up in mid-season by the San Diego Padres, he again failed to make it through spring training camp this year, but is now on the roster of the Minnesota Twins – which brings him face to face with his former teammates. But it wasn't his pitching arm that made Roy Lee so important to teammates like Barfield, Lloyd Moseby and Tony Fernandez. For Barfield and Moseby, Jackson's most important save came on a night when the Jays weren't playing – the evening Marla remembers so well – June 28, 1982.

From the first day he hung his glove in his locker in the Blue Jays' clubhouse, his fellow Jays knew there was something different about Roy Lee Jackson. From his opening days in spring training in 1981, he knew his fellow players were watching him, especially two guys named Barfield and Moseby. Jackson says, "a lot of times they'd kid with me. They knew I didn't smoke or curse or listen to rock music." Instead, Jackson's tape player usually broadcast gospel music; and whenever he got near a guitar, Roy Lee would pick it up and begin to sing songs about God!

Jackson remembers that "Jesse was somewhat puzzled. But he started watching me. He told me later that he knew there was 'something different about that guy.' "

The difference was that Roy Lee Jackson was a born-again Christian. He had become a Christian during his career with the New York Mets in 1980. Fellow Met hurler Ray Burris had invited Roy Lee to attend a Bible study, and Jackson reluctantly went along, not knowing what to expect and was determined not to do anything rash. But the experience changed his life; he asked Jesus Christ to be Lord of his life and began to learn about the new life he had found. It wasn't long before Jackson knew as much about the Bible as he does about baseball.

When he was traded to the Jays, he came with an urgent desire to share his new-found way of life with his fellow Blue Jays. Roy Lee's wife Mary had become a Christian only days following the change in her husband, and she began to share the peace and joy she had found with the wives of some of her husband's teammates, including Marla Barfield.

The Barfields initially weren't receptive. Roy Lee frankly admits, "they both used to think we were weird."

After his close friendship with Burris on the Met squad, Roy Lee found his isolation in Toronto hard to handle. He says, "It was sort of lonely. For about two weeks, I prayed for companionship on this team."

And then came the life-changing evening for the Barfields. The Jacksons followed Burris's lead and invited Jesse and Marla, along with Lloyd and Adrienne Moseby, to their home for a Bible study. None of them really wanted to go, but the Barfields knew they needed an answer, and fast, for their crumbling marriage, so they turned up with the Mosebys at the Jackson's door in Toronto.

They heard what they knew they needed: the solution to the problems that were threatening their marriages and disrupting their lives.

Marla says that until that evening she and Jesse had no idea what to do to save their marriage. But that night they turned over their lives, problems and all, to Jesus Christ. She smiles hugely: "It sure has made a difference – everything has gotten better, 100 percent better!" She reflects on the fact that in the eyes of most people Jesse and Marla Barfield have everything anyone could want – talent, popularity, wealth, fame. But she says, "Regardless of

21

the money you make, you still have that void in your life – you try to buy happiness, but it's just not there."

That's all changed. Jesse talks a lot these days about joy. Before the evening with the Jacksons he says, "I had no joy at all." Now, "joy sticks with you whatever happens."

Barfield realizes that the thing about Roy Lee that puzzled him was the joy that stuck with Roy Lee at all times: "I saw a great deal of joy in Roy Lee."

Marla believes that God brought the Barfields to Toronto so they would be in the Jackson living room on that special night. And she also believes that they're with the team to share the joy they've found with other players and their families. The Barfield family lives in Toronto through the baseball season but they make their permanent home in Houston, Texas. In both places they are actively involved in Christian fellowship – the baseball chapel during season (when it's almost impossible to attend a regular church service) and their home church in Houston in the off-season.

That's not to say that baseball has become unimportant to the MVP. Jesse believes, in fact, that being a Christian has boosted his potential. He doesn't think that God is giving him extra talent or an unfair advantage on the field. Instead, he talks about the improvement in his attitude and the concentration that his inner peace allows him at the plate and in the field.

He says, "God has blessed us with skills, and we have to refine those skills. Attitude has a lot to do with it, to be honest with you. If you approach anything with a good attitude, it's going to benefit you."

That doesn't mean that Jesse gives no credit to God for his specific accomplishments in the game. David Fisher, volunteer chaplain to the Blue Jays, remembers a booming Barfield hit in the last game of the 1984 season. There was a friendly rivalry between Jesse and first baseman Willie Upshaw for the home run leadership that year, and Jesse came to the plate trailing Upshaw by one – he had hit 26 homers, Upshaw 27. Barfield stepped to the plate and powered a key homer over his familiar right field wall. As he circled the bases, he did so with one finger pointing upward. While the fans probably interpreted that as the familiar "we're number one!" sign (hardly true in '84), Fisher, sitting in the stands, knew that Jesse was giving symbolic credit to God for everything he had accomplished.

Nor is Jesse's faith a substitute for hard work and practice. He's constantly seeking ways to improve and working hard at it. The effort doesn't always bring the desired results – his spring training experiments with different batting stances led to an eventual return to the approach he had begun with – but he's always seeking improvement.

Jesse believes that many people have a false concept of what it means to be a Christian, just as he once did. "A lot of people say we're passive. That's not true. I think it's brought out the best in me. And you'd have to experience it for yourself to understand fully what I'm talking about. It's like a verse of Scripture that says, 'Taste and see that the Lord is good.' I can tell you anything, but until you experience it for yourself, you won't know what it's like."

There is certainly nothing "passive" about Barfield's approach to his chosen game. He's aggressive at the plate, so much so that his mighty swings for the fence often result in a dramatic and dissapointing strike-out. He charges full-tilt in pursuit of fly balls and has become intimately associated with the walls and even the right-field bleachers on the occasions when his chase has taken him to – and past – the boundaries of the diamond.

But in Toronto, home of the usually lacklustre Maple Leafs' hockey team, the issue of Christian passivity is still hot. Maple Leafs' owner Harold Ballard has traded players such as Laurie Boschman (now of the Winnipeg Jets) because they became born-again Christians, and he has banned athlete evangelist Mel Stevens from the Maple Leafs' dressing room. The interest in born-again athletes has logically carried over to the Blue Jays, where players like Barfield may be giving the best answer to the skepticism of such sports bosses as Ballard and cynical members of the media.

Barfield has no intention of keeping quiet about the answers he's found. He says, "You can't help it – you can't smother this. It's just a natural thing." But he's also determined that his words will be totally backed up by his actions on and off the baseball diamond. He believes he's helped in this because his relationship with Jesus has changed his life and modified his personality: "I'm taking on the Lord's personality more than my old personality. I like that. I'm a lot more friendly towards people. I think I have more compassion for people."

He believes that he doesn't have to carry the responsibility for a "Christian" lifestyle on his own. His relationship with Christ gives him far more strength than he possesses in that muscular throwing arm.

He says, "As long as you keep yourself in the Word and in God, He won't let you slip. I mean, I'm not perfect, but I'm a lot better person than I used to be. God has helped me to understand things. He's opened my eyes spiritually to a lot of things. People are always going to hassle you, but I understand where it's coming from, and that doesn't bother me any more. I just go out and flow with it."

Despite the special camaraderie among the members of the Jays who call themselves "born again", there's a genuine family sense among almost everyone on the team. That's grown because the outspoken Christians and their teammates have a real respect for one another and because Barfield and his chapel mates have learned to deal with the issue. Jesse says, "The relationships on this team are really good, I think. One thing I've learned: you can't beat Christianity into anybody. You can't Bible-thump them.

"I think people need to see through example that we're serious Christians and that we're not going to beat them over the head with the Bible and not try to make them feel like we're holier than they are."

Nonetheless, Barfield isn't silent about his faith. David Fisher remembers one post-game media huddle centred around Barfield, who was seated at his locker. Fisher says, "Jesse started giving credit where it was due, giving glory to the Lord, and the guys started a mass exodus because it was plain to see that Jesse was just going to talk about Jesus." Barfield watched them leave, then grabbed John Robertson, baseball writer for The Toronto Sun. He said to the reporter, "Stay here! Let's talk about this. What's wrong with me giving credit to Jesus when He's the one who gave me the ability to play?"

Robertson listened, wrote the story, and has consistently been fair and objective in his articles about the Jays who talk about their faith in Jesus Christ.

Jerry Haworth, who broadcasts Toronto Blue Jays games for the Telemedia Sports Radio network, is outspoken in his praise for the Toronto right fielder. He lauds Barfield's talents on the field: "Jesse some day will be one of the game's great right fielders. Many baseball scouts now feel he has the strongest and most accurate arm in the game, shades maybe of Roberto Clemente or Dave Parker when he was in his prime." But Haworth is even more positive about the private Jesse Barfield.

Haworth says, "Jesse's make-up is outstanding. He's one of the most mature young men I've ever met. When you talk about Christian athletes, this is somebody who's a Christian, who doesn't advertise it, but who leads by example on and off the field." And Haworth, the father of two boys, adds the ultimate tribute a parent could give: "If I were going to have my sons grow up to emulate anybody in particular, it would be Jesse Barfield."

Jesse takes no credit for the changes in himself or in his marriage. He knows that the peace and joy he now possesses are gifts from God, and he says that the improvements in his family life are strictly because of the Lord's presence in the Barfield home. His approach to raising children he credits to insight from God: "It's tough raising children these days, no doubt. But you have to realize that you have to raise them, not with fear but with compassion. You have to understand where they're coming from. That's one thing the Lord has shown me: 'Put yourself in Joshua's shoes; put yourself in Jessica's shoes,' and by doing that you can understand them a lot better, understand where they're coming from. That way you won't be too harsh on them."

Jesse works as hard at maintaining his strong faith as he does when hitting the weight room to build up his physical strength. He says that the biggest growth factor for him is reading the Bible: "The more you get into the Bible, the more you want to get into the Bible. There are times when nothing else will do. When something's bothering me I go to the Word, and I have a peace within me, knowing that the answer's already there. The only thing I have to do is to seek Him out for it. When that happens, everything else falls into place."

The first verse in the Bible that Jesse would turn to might be from the first letter of John, chapter four, verse four. He quotes it from memory: "You are of God, little children, and have overcome them, because greater is He that is in you than he that is in the world." He says that this reminds him that, whatever the circumstances he finds himself in, God is there, and God is greater than the problem: "It's funny about Christians. Some of them think that they won't go through trials and tribulations. They're wrong – they will. But God said, that when you go through them, He'll be with you. It's a good assurance, knowing that in everything I do and everywhere I go, He's with me no matter what."

He also says that having several fellow Christians on the team is a tremendous asset in his Christian development. No longer would Jackson have to pray for a born-again friend on the club; there are now enough to field a team! Jesse acknowledges that God has done something special in the locker room. He says, "It's just a phenomenal thing. God has enabled us to reach out and touch a lot of people, and that's fantastic."

The public and media attention on the Blue Jays is not likely to decrease in 1986. The man in the right field spotlight has two commitments this year: to live for God and to play his heart out for his ball club. Like everyone around Exhibition Stadium in Toronto, Barfield believes the club can go even farther than the American League East championship. He'd like to pick up that pennant on the way to the World Series, and he believes the Blue Jays can accomplish that by being even better than in '85.

He argues, "Last year we were good. I think we have the capability of being a great ball club. We had guys who had mediocre years. I had a great year, and I think I'm capable of having an even better year. If we get a few more guys on track, that's all the baseball world's going to be talking about for the next few years: the Blue Jays!"

It's obvious that Jesse's first goal is a team goal. Despite the acclaim that he earned during his great 1985 season, he says that the highlight for him was the team's collective accomplishment: "Getting to the playoffs last year was one of the biggest moments in my career so far. If we had won the whole thing that would have been even better. But getting that respectability around the whole league and across the nation, that's been tremendous."

Many observers argue that, because the Jays are playing the American game north of the border, the level of respect is still far below the appropriate level. John Robertson has written, "They may turn out to be the only World Champions in the history of baseball to wear unlisted numbers." About Barfield he asked, "How big would Jesse Barfield be in New York or Los Angeles, with 27 homers, 84 RBIs, a league-leading 21 outfield assists and 22 stolen bases?"

Jesse is dedicated to playing his part in the continued improvement of the Blue Jays. When he's congratulated on his great 1985 season, he quietly disagrees! He contends, "A lot of people have come up to me and said, 'You had a great year, Jesse.' Deep down inside I know I didn't have a great year. I had a good year. And this year I'm looking forward to having a great year. Last year I set goals for myself, and I reached almost everyone of those goals. Now I have to set goals even higher for myself to compete within myself. I think that by getting more at bats – and I think that's going to happen this year – I can produce more and have bigger numbers: 35 home runs, a .300-plus batting average and 100 or more runs batted in."

Is he going to accomplish this with intense concentration and professional grit? Probably. But he also admits, "I just go out there and have fun. Baseball is definitely a lot of fun."

"The money is nice. There's nothing wrong with having money, but money doesn't make you a better person. God makes you a better person, through Jesus Christ."

Chapter 3

Lloyd Moseby

It's just about game time, and the usually taciturn Willie Upshaw is turning his locker upside down. "I can't find my game glove!" he moans. "Has anybody seen it?"

There are, of course, several other gloves in the pile of equipment that has been turned out of the locker, but none of them will do – he always plays with his "gamer."

A few lockers away teammate Lloyd Moseby is leaning back, smile on his face, observing Willie's consternation from the corner of his eye. Something clicks in Willie's mind, and he fires an accusation at the centre fielder. Lloyd's face is a study in innocence. "Willie, would I do a thing like that?"

Willie knows the answer to that question and patiently awaits until his buddy coughs up the glove. Moseby later admits that he phrased his answer that way because, "I can't lie." He also confesses that this is probably the hundredth time he's hidden Upshaw's glove or his shoes. Willie knows that's one of the prices you pay for a close friendship with one of the most upbeat, positive guys on the Toronto Blue Jays baseball club.

Lloyd Moseby loves baseball. He especially loves playing baseball in the big leagues, in the uniform (number 15) of the Toronto Blue Jays. Asked about the high points of his already illustrious career, he looks back to the day he put on that uniform for the first time.

"The highlight of my career was coming up to the Jays. Garth Iorg, Louis Leal and I all came to the Jays the same day." The call-up had come as something of a surprise, and the players flew into Toronto International Airport barely in time to make the game that day – May 24, 1980. Lloyd remembers it well: "We were late. We were taken with a police escort to the ball park. When we got there, Bobby Mattick (then the manager and now Blue Jays vice-president) threw me into the ball game against pitcher Tommy John."

Moseby was awestruck. He had watched from the bleachers when John pitched in the World Series for the Los Angeles Dodgers. His first thought was "I can't believe I'm here, let alone be playing against Tommy John!" But his second thought was "Hit the ball!" And he did. Moseby smacked a home run in his major league debut and drove in four runs to help the Blue Jays to victory that day.

The next afternoon, Moseby was at the plate again, this time against another noted veteran pitcher, Luis Tiant. Again he hit the ball well, with two hits in four times at bat, including a double, and he batted in two more runs. His major league career was off to a great start. Lloyd describes it with what is probably his favourite word: "Tremendous!"

But it didn't stay tremendous. He remembers, "Immediately after that, I went downhill. That was a tough year mentally for me."

Moseby had faced adversity before, as far back as his Little League days. He wanted to play catcher for a team in his home town of Oakland, California, but the future major league star was cut from the squad. (The coach who made that insightful decision must feel a little like the record companies that originally turned down the Beatles because they obviously had nothing going for them). That didn't stop Lloyd, though; he was determined to make it in baseball, at his favourite position, crouched behind home plate. When his managers and coaches insisted that he play in the outfield, he was unhappy. He also admits that he wasn't very good.

"When I came up from high school, they put me in centre field. I was terrible. But I was a pretty good catcher. I always thought of myself as a catcher, and I was proud of it. That's where I learned to play the game. But they said, 'Your legs are too good, you run too fast, so we'll put you at first base.' Then, I was terrible there. But finally, I learned how to play first base. Now, I was a good first baseman."

"And then the Blue Jays drafted me and they put me in the outfield. I'd never played in the outfield until I came to the Jays. Now, I'm a terrible outfielder! I took a hundred fly balls a day at practice. Jesse Barfield would come every morning and laugh at me, taking all those extra flies. After the practice I was usually tired and mad."

"Then they switched me to right field. Now, I'm a terrible right fielder, because the ball spins differently in right field. I caught – or tried to catch – another hundred fly balls a day, in instructional ball. They also made me do diving practice. I'm the only guy I know who had to have diving practice where I literally dove at the ground to take a sinking fly."

32

"And then all of a sudden they say, 'Rick Bosetti is going to be leaving the organization. Lloyd can play centre.' So now, here I am in centre field. And I'm a terrible centre fielder, all over again. My whole baseball career has been one learning experience after another. I guess that's why I'm a pretty strong individual.

"I think I'm a pretty decent centre fielder now. I just wonder when they're going to put me at shortstop."

This season he's not at short stop. Tony Fernandez seems to have a lock on that position in the infield. But Moseby has seen another change; he was moved at the start of the season to the lead-off position in the batting order. He's responded well to the change, hitting at a torrid pace in the opening games, waiting out walks and stealing bases. He insists that his lead-off role won't diminish his aggressiveness, and wants the right to swing away at 3-and-0 (three balls, no strikes) pitches, instead of following the usual lead-off pattern of taking the next pitch instead of trying to eke out a walk.

The lead-off spot should give him opportunity for one of his offensive loves – stealing bases. He stole 39 in 1984, two less in '85 – significant achievements for a man of Moseby's stature, six feet three inches, and two hundred well-proportioned pounds. He charges second on an attempted steal, sliding fingers- and head-first into the bag for a very positive success ratio – and no broken fingers or nose yet to show for the extra effort. His best qualification for lead-off hitting is probably the notorious Moseby confidence.

Since opening day, Lloyd has moved up and down in the batting order, but wherever they place him, he has hit well.

The stories of his enforced experiments at half of the positions on the diamond, as told by Lloyd Moseby, may be true, but they are offered with the same self-deprecating humour that is his trademark. There's no doubt that he's more than "pretty decent" at centre field. Barfield, who admits that he found an unfair amount of amusement in Lloyd's extra catching and diving practice, finds nothing to laugh at now. About Moseby, he says, "He struggled a little bit at first. But if you look at Lloyd Moseby today compared to a few years ago, what a difference! He's a tremendous (Jesse may have picked up that term from Lloyd) outfielder now."

There were probably times during diving practice that Lloyd wished he was back on the basketball court. The two sports – baseball and basketball – were the twin loves of his life as he grew up in Oakland. He was named All-American in both sports while in high school and earned his nickname, "Shaker" (which is now monogrammed on his personalized, "Powerized" Louisville Slugger "125" bats), from his ability to deke opponents on the basketball court.

The scales began to tip toward baseball in the first years of high school. Lloyd played both sports in grade nine, but in grade ten he made the momentous decision to bypass basketball and concentrate on baseball. He now says, "It had to be one of the dumbest things I did in all my career," not because he'd rather be playing basketball, but because there was really no need to make the decision at that stage of his life. He actually returned to basketball in subsequent years.

But that grade ten decision established his career

priorities, and Lloyd credits his high school coach with guidance throughout those years (Lloyd is always quick with praise for his mentors, from his Mom to Bobby Mattick to his current coaches, manager and teammates). His secondary school coach saw that Lloyd's superior talent lay in baseball, and Moseby will admit that his year of concentrated baseball gave him a better chance to learn the fundamentals of the game.

The conflict between chasing balls to the foul line or shooting baskets from the foul line remained, however. He says, "I continued to play two sports and fortunately for me, I was drafted very high, in the first round (second pick overall) by the Blue Jays. I had a decision to make, whether to go to college on a basketball/baseball scholarship or to sign with the Jays and help my parents out."

The tension between two sports was nothing new for the Blue Jays. Infielder Danny Ainge had played under an agreement that also allowed him to play basketball, and eventually he moved to the Boston Celtics, where he is now a star with the best squad in professional basketball. Moseby made the opposite choice. He now plays very little basketball, especially because (since the departure of Ainge) the game has been banned as an off-hours recreation during training camp. Lloyd understands the decision was made to minimize off-field injuries to high-priced baseball players, but he mourns the loss of his number two sporting love all the same.

His ultimate decision was governed by a concern for his family, which includes four brothers and three sisters. He says, "We didn't have a whole lot of money. We didn't have a whole lot of anything –

but I always had tennis shoes and cleats on my feet and nice clothes on my body. My Mom went without those things for years; I would see the same coat for eight or nine years, the same shoes for five or six. My dream was always to help my parents out, to get them out of that situation. I had the opportunity, and I took it."

Although he didn't make it to Toronto in his first season (1978), he did play in Canada – he joined the Medicine Hat Blue Jays in the Pioneer League, where he was named to the All-Star squad. In 1979 he was with Dunedin and in 1980 played briefly in Syracuse until he was called up to the big club in May.

Moseby rebounded from his poor rookie season to lead the club in a number of categories in 1981. He was the top Blue Jay in runs scored (36), hits (88) and total bases (135), and he tied for the lead in RBIs (43) and game-winning RBIs (6). In September of that year he married Adrienne; they now have two children, Alicia and Lloyd Jr.

But with everything apparently coming together on the field, in reality Lloyd was coming apart inside. He tells the story this way: "Things were going well. In signing with a big league ball club I have most of the things that I guess most people would probably want out of life – a car, a good job, a family.

"But there was a void there. I didn't know what it was, but I knew that there was an unhappiness and an uneasiness about my life-style. There was something there that wasn't right."

Moseby now understands how he could have been in such an envied position and still be unhappy: "It's the world's depression. It didn't have anything to do with money or fame. It's waking up in the morning and not being pleased with something inside you. I think anybody who reads this will realize what the problem was."

Like Jesse and Marla Barfield, Lloyd and Adrienne found the perfect answer to fill that void one evening at the apartment of Roy Lee and Mary Jackson.

Lloyd expresses Jackson's interest in baseball terminology: "Even the year before, Roy Lee was tagging at me." Moseby was afraid that Jackson was going to register a put-out if he ever connected, and he kept trying to convince himself that he was really doing all right without the kind of things Jackson was into.

"I always went to chapel, just like most people go to church. But after church or after chapel I was back to the old things I used to do, and that void still remained. Roy would invite me out to dinner and share the Word of God with me, but after he did that I'd forget about what he'd said.

"Actually, I really didn't want to get mixed up with him, because I knew I wouldn't be able to go to the clubs, and I wouldn't be able to do the things I used to do. I tried to stay as far away from Roy Lee as I could.

"But one particular day I was really on the down side. It seemed as if nothing was going right, and I didn't want to talk to anybody. I just wanted to be left alone.

"But then I saw Roy Lee – he was laughing and having a ball. I knew that he seemed to be in a good mood almost all the time."

Suddenly Lloyd discovered that he really did want to understand Jackson's secret. He says, "I wanted to know what was going on, how I could get some fulfillment out of my life." He knew he couldn't ask these questions of many of the people he'd met as a ballplayer; he felt he couldn't trust most of those people because they seemed to be interested in Moseby for the benefits it brought to them – financial opportunities, vicarious fame or simply good tickets to the next Blue Jays' home game. He also knew that that wasn't true of Roy Lee Jackson.

"I found Roy Lee and asked him some questions about God. He really gave me some solid answers. I think that was the key – I got some good answers. If he hadn't answered in a way that suited my needs, I don't know where I'd be today; if it weren't for Roy Lee Jackson sharing the Word with me, I don't think that today I'd be where I am right now."

Jackson invited Moseby to the Bible study at his home. Lloyd says, "On that day, I gave my life up to the Lord. Oh, not completely, I wouldn't say it was that easy. I won't say that at that time my life changed overnight, but I will say that I found that there was somebody who really cared about me in spite of all the negative things I was doing. As time progressed, I came to know a personal relationship with the Lord. I knew that the Lord loved me, and I knew that I had the ability to repent and to love my enemies as well as my brothers."

Like Barfield, Moseby doesn't believe God gave him an injection of athletic talent just because he became a born-again Christian. But Lloyd also agrees with his right-fielder friend, contending that he's a better ballplayer because he's a Christian.

He says, "There's no question about it. For example, we can go back to the play-offs. I'd never been in a situation like that before, even though we'd just played a game against the Yankees that was a pretty important game, almost like a World Series game.

"Those are the kinds of games where your nervous system really just breaks down. Your enthusiasm is above normal, your heart rate is above normal – and these are serious things.

"But I think for me at that particular time, I played the game in a more low-keyed, more stable condition than I'd ever played before. It was a matter of going out and praising the Lord and doing what I did all through the season. I concentrated on giving God the glory, I went 0 for 10 in my first 10 at-bats, but sooner or later things did break for me. But I think I can say that I didn't change my attitude after they broke."

Barfield has argued that being a Christian doesn't destroy the healthy, aggressive attitude that's so necessary to being a good athlete. Moseby also contends, unlike common stereotypes might suggest, that being a Christian doesn't rob you of your sense of humour and enjoyment of fun. You don't need to be around Lloyd Moseby for very long to see convincing evidence of that. Just ask Willie Upshaw!

Moseby admits that he enjoys practical jokes. "I've done about a million of them. I just like having fun. I think that's one of the most important things about being a Christian. If you lose your sense of humour in anything – not just baseball, but in any everyday job – I think you're in for a lot of trouble, because Satan is going around seeking whom he may devour, and if he can catch you with your spirits low, he's got a very good opportunity to attack."

In the high pressure and inflated-egos world of professional sports, may athletes face the problem of an overblown sense of their own importance. When everyone tells you you're wonderful, it's hard, after a while, not to believe them. Of course, when the media and the fans begin to call you a bum, that's hard to ignore as well. A lot of athletes claim that they don't read the papers or watch sportscasts, but they can't deafen their ears to the cheers or boos from the bleachers.

Lloyd believes that his faith has helped him put his self-esteem into a more realistic perspective. "I think being a Christian gives you the ability to laugh at yourself. That was something I wasn't able to do before I got saved. I took the game extremely seriously. I still do, but on a different basis now.

"When I go on the field now, I'm playing for the Lord, so I try to be sure everybody can see how happy I am, to let the joy that's in me flow out. No matter if I make an error or a great play, I try to have the same kind of humour within me."

Broadcaster Jerry Haworth has commented on Moseby's humour, positive attitude and determination to play full-out for the Jays at all times. He says: "Lloyd is very outgoing. He's confident. When he came to the Blue Jays in 1980 as a 20-year-old kid, he was just thrown into the fire and had to fend for himself. I think that during those three straight seasons when he hit .230, and as he had to learn the hard way at the major league level, it was his Christianity that kept him going.

"He's the most positive thinker on the ball club; he never lets himself get down. And Jimy Williams knows, and before him Bobby Cox knew that Lloyd gives 100 percent whether they bat him first or ninth, play him left, centre or right. They can count on a great, responsible effort, because he's a responsible young man."

Moseby is quick to admit that he wasn't an instant success as a Christian. It's taken effort and time for him to grow in his new faith. He believes that the companionship of others who share his beliefs has been the major factor which has helped him to remain true to his commitment to God and to mature as a believer.

He especially points to Jesse Barfield and Ron Shepherd as key ingredients in what Christians call "fellowship" – friendship that goes beyond having fun, to the place where the friends can talk seriously about the situations they face in life and can pray together and study the Bible together. But he also maintains contact with the guy who tagged him with a Bible, Roy Lee Jackson. Lloyd says, "Talking to Roy on occasion, as I do, helps me tremendously."

Spending time with other believers is always an important boost, according to the centre fielder. "I know they're in the same boat as I am, living day to day."

He believes there's a danger in trying to suspend time and experience back in the Jackson's living room, staying at the point when he first surrendered his life to Jesus. "That's not going to save me today. I have a lot of day-to-day problems like anyone else. It's a day-to-day battle.

"I think talking about the Word and speaking the Word and trying to keep each other uplifted in the name of Jesus are the most important things we can do in our daily walk."

But Moseby is always careful not to sound too holy or to preach as though he's got it made. He continued, "I'd be the first one to admit that I don't do that every day." For Lloyd, as for any other professional ballplayer, it's easy to find all of his time taken up with his sport and his fame. There's always one more reporter to talk to after a game, and many of the players find their media jousts much more tiring than the actual nine innings on the diamond.

Adrienne often welcomes home a very exhausted husband, and her husband admits that it's easy just to sink into a kind of mental oblivion, stretch out on the long Moseby couch and forget about the priorities that he knows are so important to his everyday growth and positive attitude.

"By the time I get home, I'm so mentally drained by questions and by baseball that I make the excuse that I'm tired. I immediately lie down and forget what I should be doing, which is reading the Bible and uplifting my spirit. That's actually the single most important thing a person can do."

Moseby also says that Christians need to spend time talking to God, in prayer. Again, he admits his own failures: "I don't do as much as I should. We should pray more, we should intercede for each other, we should pray for others, even though they don't ask us to."

He gives an example close to the heart of the Christian believers on the Blue Jays. At the time this was written, Ron Shepherd was the only one of those involved in this book who was not playing for the parent club. His centre-field buddy thinks this should be a matter for prayer: "We should pray for Ron Shepherd. He's having a tough time getting on the club, and we should pray for him. The Lord wants us to uplift one another."

Neither Moseby nor Shepherd would argue that God will instantly find Ron a place on the squad, and that's not the reason for their prayers. Instead, they recognize that the inner peace that God is eager to supply is an important ingredient in handling any situation that comes along. Shepherd may play in Syracuse or sign with another major league club, like Roy Lee Jackson. His friends on the Jays would love to see him make it in the majors, but more than anything they want to be sure that Shepherd knows God's peace and joy in whatever circumstance he finds himself.

Moseby would not pretend to understand everything about how God works. He doesn't even claim to understand everything about how Lloyd Moseby ticks. And he believes that the learning process is an integral part of Christian living.

"I think that we're all learning and that we're supposed to keep right on learning until the day the Lord comes back. He's teaching us His way, now, through Paul and through David and through all the apostles in the Bible."

But when asked for his favourite section from the Bible, he doesn't quote David or Paul or any of the apostles. He turns instead to the book of the prophet Isaiah, who wrote about the life and death of Jesus hundreds of years before Jesus was born:

"Who hath believed our report? and to whom is the arm of the Lord revealed? For He shall grow up before Him as a tender plant, and as a root out of a dry ground: He hath no form nor comeliness; and when we shall see Him, there is no beauty that we should desire Him. He is despised and rejected of men; a man of sorrows, and acquainted with grief: and we hid as it were our faces from Him; He was despised, and we esteemed Him not.

"Surely He hath borne our griefs, and carried our sorrows: yet we did esteem Him stricken, smitten of God, and afflicted. But He was wounded for our transgressions, He was bruised for our iniquities: the chastisement of our peace was upon Him; and with His stripes we are healed. All we like sheep have gone astray; we have turned every one to his own way; and the Lord hath laid on Him the iniquity of us all. He was oppressed, and He was afflicted, yet He opened not His mouth: He is brought as a lamb to the slaughter, and as a sheep before her shearers is dumb, so He openeth not His mouth" (Isaiah 53:1-7).

It's a surprising passage, coming from a ballplayer who is noted for his practical jokes, quick smile and consistent sense of humour. But Moseby believes it's a crucial section of Scripture, for two reasons. First, because it tells the story of the great love that caused Jesus to take our sin and our sickness upon Himself: "Isaiah had a vision of this man, a man who was going to come one day and who was going to be like a sacrificial lamb, shedding His blood for us."

Second, it's important because of the opening question: "Who has believed the report?" Moseby asks himself that same question almost every day. "I ask myself, 'Do you believe that report? Is that report in your heart?' If so, I have to go out and live that report and tell that report. When I read the Bible and understand it, why should I keep it to myself? How can I be so selfish as to hold everything inside, to say, 'OK I've got it now, this is mine'?

"We have to go out and share what we've found. And it doesn't have to be to some far-away, missionary place like Egypt or somewhere. We have to go into our own back yard. It might mean going down the street. It might be in church, or talking to a hooker on the street corner, or in baseball chapel. It might be anywhere, but there are people right here that need the Word."

David Fisher remembers an incident which shows that Moseby and company are quite prepared to put their mouths where their hearts are: "Two summers ago, a church in Toronto was celebrating an 80th anniversary. The guy in charge of the celebration called the Blue Jays and asked if some players could come. The Jays put him in touch with me, as chapel coordinator.

"I asked Roy Lee Jackson and Jesse and Lloyd, and they all agreed. We were invited to a Sunday morning breakfast, so I picked them up at 7 a.m. and we went to the church.

As soon as we arrived, they were besieged by autograph seekers. It didn't seem like a church at all, and the guys were just being mobbed. Suddenly Lloyd said, 'Hey, we didn't come here to sign autographs; we came here to worship the Lord! Maybe when we're done we'll sign, but we have to talk about Jesus this morning.'

"So we had breakfast, and then the master of ceremonies – former Toronto Maple Leaf Jim McKenny – introduced the three players, and one by one they came up to the podium and shared their testimonies. That morning, Lloyd plainly stated what he believed. He told them that if they didn't accept Jesus into their lives, they would go to hell! While he was speaking, Jesse and Roy kept whispering, 'Preach it, brother, preach!' All three of them laid their faith right on the line that day. It was beautiful!"

Fisher says that Lloyd's words on that occasion were possible because he is very familiar with what the Bible has to say about the necessity of knowing

45

Christ: "You just have to look at Lloyd's Bible when he's in chapel. He has this little burgundy Bible that's marked up and highlighted all the way through. The same with Jesse – when Jesse talks, the scriptures are just flowing out of him because they're in him, alive and working. Their words aren't some shallow testimony, the kind you find with many ballplayers."

Many observers of the athletic world would contend that someone who spends that much time studying the Bible is going to see a corresponding decline in his abilities and his concentration. Blue Jay manager Jimy Williams obviously has no such complaint about his everyday centre fielder, whom one Toronto sports writer has called "a fixture" in the Jays' defensive line-up. He says, "Lloyd is in very good physical condition, and his mental frame of mind is excellent."

It's because the Blue Jays brass have such a high opinion of Moseby that they moved him to the crucial lead-off spot in the line-up. First Jay on the line, every day, is Lloyd Moseby. Williams thinks that, like the rest of the club, Lloyd is hungry to go beyond the success of 1985.

The Blue Jays' manager says, "I don't think any of us are really satisfied with the accomplishments in 1985, even though they were extensive. I think there's a bigger and better carrot out there that we're definitely striving to attain. We're going to do our best to attain it, through hard work on [Lloyd's] part and the rest of the ball club."

Lloyd certainly intends to give it his best shot in 1986. He says that he doesn't set numerical goals; instead, he'll be striving with all of his concentration for a trait he found elusive in 1985 – consistency. He says, "Consistency is the key to my

46

game. If I can get off to a fast start" – and he certainly has done so in the spring of '86 – "things are going to be tremendous. Last year I got off to a slow start, but I had the ability not to get mentally shaken by the whole deal. I stayed with myself, and I tried to uplift others."

Faced with a slump, many athletes become withdrawn and silent. Moseby deliberately reacts by taking exactly the opposite tack. He says, "I think that was the key for me. Instead of going around crying about Lloyd Moseby and how I'm not doing well, I kept trying to uplift the guys who were doing well into having even better seasons. Jesse was having a good year, and I kept on clapping and shaking his hand and motivating him to keep going.

"Tony Fernandez was having a good year, and I kept trying to uplift him, knowing that sooner or later my time would come. And when it did come, my attitude again never changed. It was as if I was already hitting .400 the entire season.

"I think our walk is important. If I go out and talk to some kids and tell them that the Lord wants us to be happy and then I go 0 for 20 and start crying in the newspaper, I'm contradicting myself."

Moseby had a chance to put his personal "theory of Christian attitudes" on the line in the final series against the New York Yankees in the tense windup to 1985. On October 4 the Blue Jays were set to clinch the pennant on the third-to-last day of the season and went into the ninth inning ahead. A routine fly ball was popped into centre field, and it fell into – and out of – Lloyd Moseby's glove. Well over 40,000 fans gasped collectively, and the Yanks went on to win the game, 4-3.

For one evening, anyway, the popular centre fielder was the goat, although the loyal Toronto fans were extremely kind to him, even applauding his next appearance at the plate.

Moseby admits that the experience shook him. He calls it "one of the most depressing, awful times of my life." Yet while he stood on the field and sat in the dug-out in the Jay's half of the ninth, he allowed God's peace to calm him. By the time he got to the dressing room, he was ready to meet the reporters.

"I wasn't joyful or laughing about it, but I was telling them, 'Hey, I've dropped balls before,'" which was exactly the same answer fellow Blue Jays and management were giving to the same question, all admitting their own errors. That kind of mutual support is one of the factors that moulds the Jays into a great team.

By the time Lloyd got home that night – to an empty house, because Adrienne and the kids had returned home to California, since she was in school – the emotional impact had taken over again. As Lloyd put through a long-distance call to California, he admits, "I was devastated; I was hurt."

The next morning Lloyd picked up his Bible and began to read. He remembers the peace that was his that morning: "The next day the Lord showed me, through His Word, that He would never leave me or forsake me." The man who had made the key error returned to Exhibition Stadium at peace and full of confidence.

Kansas City manager Dick Howser, who was watching the game closely to see if he would be facing the Jays, noticed Moseby's courage. Instead of coming to the plate tentatively, with his confidence shaken, Lloyd brought all the self-assurance he needed to swat a home run in that October 5 game, the day the Blue Jays won the American League East pennant.

The loyal Jays fans stood and cheered loud and long for their centre fielder, who had atoned for his error – but Lloyd Moseby had no doubt who should really get the credit!

If the 1986 season continues as it began for the Blue Jays' centre fielder, there will be a lot of credit coming his way. The club's decision to bat him in the lead-off spot paid major dividends, and his fielding and base running are better than ever.

But whether Lloyd Moseby is in a streak or a slump, he'll be doing his best to redirect the glory to the God who has met more needs for Lloyd than he himself will ever meet, in his best year, for the Toronto Blue Jays.

Chapter 4

Tony Fernandez

The boys on the Blue Jays' bench call Tony Fernandez "Flipper" – not that he bears any resemblance to a certain senior citizen dolphin, but because of his unique method of conveying the ball to first base. After fielding a grounder deep in the hole, behind second base, Tony usually gets it to first via his patented, wristy, underhand flip.

It's a style unique in the majors, though odds are good that a lot of young Blue Jays fans are practising the style when they take their turn at shortstop. Tony might not recommend that approach, though; his goal in 1986 is to decrease his throwing errors to first, and he's worked to develop a more conventional, foot-planted overhand strike to Willie Upshaw at first base.

If the Fernandez flip goes the way of the dinosaur, the boys on the bench can simply revert to his second nickname: "Gadgetman." He's earned that title through his love for any gimmick that might possibly give him another slight edge in his game. In the clubhouse he can constantly be seen working with small weights or other paraphernalia, a look of intensity on his dark young face.

But the serious Tony Fernandez image crumbles quickly and often, as the star shortstop from the Dominican Republic breaks into his large and frequent smile.

Tony has a lot to smile about. His talent for baseball has lifted Tony and his family out of the intense poverty he knew as a child.

Fernandez grew up in the now famous baseball town of San Pedro de Macoris, in the Dominican Republic. That one town has spawned a couple of All-Star teams of major league ball players, including Fernandez's teammate George Bell. Damaso Garcia is also a Dominican, as are several of the "junior Jays" – such players as Manny Lee, who are working their way up in the minor league system. The Blue Jays have drafted so many players from "Macoris" that Dominican citizens cheer on their Jays as loudly as do Torontonians – more enthusiastically, probably, than residents of a southern Ontario city like London, with their unpatriotic loyalties to the nearby Tigers!

The Dominican Republic occupies the eastern half of the island of Hispaniola in the Caribbean Sea; the nation's none-too-friendly western neighbour is Haiti, known as one of the poorest countries in the world. The mountains that separate the two countries guarantee a slightly better quality of life for the Dominicans, because much of the rain there falls eastward of the mountains. But, while the climate is tropical and pleasant, the land is still very poor; houses are small and very simple, and the large families often eke out a living barely above the subsistence level.

The Fernandez family was certainly large – Tony has six brothers and four sisters, who range in age from 17 years older than Tony to four years younger – and very poor. His father worked in the sugar cane fields and factories, doing whatever job was appropriate to the season. He planted and harvested sugar cane, supervised crews in the fields, and worked many hours in the processing plant. Both of Tony's parents are now dead – his mother, Andrea, died just before spring training, on Valentine's Day, 1986 – and one of his most painful memories of his father is of the toll his long, back-breaking hours took on him.

Tony recalls, "Every time I saw my father working that hard to raise his children, I almost cried. I get real sad, wondering why my father had to work that hard."

His mother tried to supplement the family income by operating a tiny grocery store in the Fernandez home, but with 13 people living under one small roof, there was little room for business.

Those circumstances gave Tony all the motivation he needed to find the best way to help his family. In San Pedro de Macoris, there were only two ways up the financial ladder – education or baseball. Tony had begun to play baseball before he was nine years old, in the streets, on the beaches or on the rock-strewn diamonds. His bats were often rough lengths of wood, and a Dominican kid would have given the shirt off his back – if he were lucky enough to own one – for the kind of baseballs the Blue Jays toss into the garbage after they've been used in the batting cage. But lack of decent equipment does nothing to cool the baseball fever in the Dominican Republic, especially since the country had already produced baseball heroes such as Cesar Cedeño and a clutch of others.

Tony frequently cut classes to get in some extra innings. His desk was often empty, as he hung ground balls every day.

Those experiences helped him with his career decision, although he's bright and probably would have succeeded in obtaining a good education. His choice was the bigger gamble because, despite the amazing number of Dominicans who've made it to the majors, there are hundreds and thousands of young men back home who watched their dream of economic freedom die at the sand lot level. One of the disappointed is Tony's twin brother, Jose, who was also signed by the Blue Jays, but who was unable to play his way off the island.

For Octavio Antonio Fernandez, even his early affection for the game produced a small financial benefit. When the stadium staff tired of trying to throw the young intruder out, they submitted to the inevitable and gave him a job on the stadium cleaning staff. That offer of work, which carried with it approved entrance to the stadium, sealed Tony's fate – baseball would be his life, and he would pursue that career as far as it would carry him.

We know how far that's been, to this point of his career – and it's surprising to realize that, despite the fame that's already his, Tony is still so new to the majors that he is yet ineligible for salary arbitration. Under league rules the club was still able to set his 1986 salary without agreement from Fernandez.

His first step to the big leagues came courtesy of Epy Guerrero, the Blue Jays' scouting legend who knows Dominican baseball as well as Buck Martinez knows the inside of his catcher's mask. He saw something special in Tony Fernandez and signed him for the Blue Jays. Tony came into the organization with an iron determination to make good his promise to his family.

The same determined spirit kept Tony at his post throughout the 1985 season, the only Blue Jay to play all 161 games. John Robertson, of the Toronto Sun, has described him as "A gentle, soft-spoken man with the reflexes of a Baryshnikov and the heart of a lion."

His perfect attendance record, which might shock the teachers in San Pedro de Macoris, held in the closing hours of the regular season, in part as a gift from manager Bobby Cox. In the final game of the season, which was virtually meaningless to the Jays but important to very-veteran Yankee pitcher Phil Niekro, who was throwing for his 300th victory, the Blue Jay team that took the field looked more like the Syracuse Chiefs. Tony was only to be seen relaxing on the bench with the other starters, while the second string took on the rival New York Yankees. But in the ninth inning, Cox sent Fernandez into the lost cause to pinch hit, a role foreign to the young shortstop. His single was one of a very few that Niekro allowed that day, but it lifted Tony's season's hitting average to near .290 (some think he has the potential to lead the league in hitting) and earned him the unofficial "Iron Man" title, the only Blue Jay to appear in 161 games.

Niekro got his 300th win – he's trying to add to that total in a Cleveland Indians' uniform this season – to the praise of teammates and Blue Jays opponents alike.

Fernandez' determination took him back to winter ball in the Dominican Republic after the '85 season, where he won the batting championship. That same spirit urges him on to become even better, and his search for aids to excellence has earned him the nickname "Gadget-man."

Some observers have already speculated that he

might be the best shortstop in the league. Jerry Haworth says, "He might be the finest fielding shortstop in the American League."

He may not yet be the best all-round infielder, but Blue Jays coach Cito Gaston points out, "Tony's a young kid. (He'll turn 24 on August 6, 1986). He's still learning and the more he plays, the better he's going to get, and the more things he's going to be able to do."

He does a lot of them awfully well now. In 1985 his usual place in the batting order was ninth. He may have been the best ninth-place hitter in the majors, turning in a more than respectable average of .289 (the best in his short major-league career), with 163 hits including 31 doubles and 10 triples – a tribute more to his speed than his power. Yet the Blue Jays' management also believes that Tony will be capable of contributing a dozen or more homers each year.

In the American League championship series against Kansas City he was even better, hitting at a .333 clip, one of the best Blue Jay play-off averages.

His success brought the benefits home that Tony had hoped for. Before his mother died, her favourite possession was a picture of her shortstop son in Blue Jay uniform, autographed with love from "Antonio." It hung on the wall in the same home Tony grew up in, although his financial success allowed his family to add seven rooms to the five-room house. He has kept his promise to help his relatives on the Caribbean island: every payday a significant chunk of the Fernandez paycheque goes directly to his family in the Dominican Republic, c/o Epy Guerrero.

Tony is an emotional young man. Like the rest of his family, he is not afraid to show his feelings, and tears come to his eyes as he says,

"Finally my dreams came true. I signed (with the Jays) when I was 16 or 17 years old; I took the chance of leaving school because I saw that my parents were getting old and I wanted to help my family. I was trying hard to be someone so I could help my parents." And although his parents have now passed away – his father did not live to see him make the majors – his mother was able to share in her son's early success.

For Fernandez, like other players wearing the Toronto uniform after growing up in warmer climates, the cold snaps that hit southern Ontario in early spring and late fall can be something of a shock. But Tony takes a positive view of the trip from palm trees and warm beaches to the parka weather of April home games. He might be a good candidate as a spokesman for a commercial promoting his summer city.

He says, "I enjoy living in Toronto, because you have to have change once in a while. Maybe for the first couple of weeks the cold weather bothers me a little bit. But I get used to it, and I like the city. It's clean and it's peaceful living there. You don't have to worry about coming into the street and finding someone who wants to rip you off. For me, Toronto's one of the best cities."

He also is full of praise for his Blue Jays team. He says, "I think it's one of the best clubs to play for, because the players and the staff get along real well. And when you get along with the people, that helps you a lot. I don't think there are any big differences between anyone, from the coaching staff to the players. We respect the coaches and we have confidence in them, but we feel free to talk to them. It's good when you can trust someone in your club.

In an ironic sense, when Tony moved to Toronto he moved very close to his home and his family. Tony's parents raised him in an intensely Christian family. Both father and mother were devout believers in Christ, but their son had little time for faith – he was much more interested in fielding. Yet since Tony joined the Toronto Blue Jays, he has returned to the faith held so intensely by his mother and father, and he is now so committed to living as a born-again Christian that any conversation with the young Dominican is full of references to his faith and praise to God – so much so that many writers tend to shy away from in-depth interviews with him.

It wasn't an easy decision for Tony to come to. As he admits, he desperately wanted to be a "someone," and his rapid advance through the minor leagues made it obvious he had every chance to become a superstar. Perhaps he associated Christianity with the kind of desperate poverty he'd left behind; perhaps he felt he no longer needed a Christian church, because he was doing just fine on his own, thank you.

Tony describes his development this way:

"My father was a Christian for 40 years, so I was born into the Christian life. I used to go to church, and our father used to teach us about Christ when I was a little kid. I was reading about Christ since I was a little kid. But when I grew up, I took the wrong way. When I was 14 or 15 years old, I turned away."

But it's difficult to abandon the heritage left you by a loving family; and a longing for the faith he'd seen in his mother and father followed him through his minor league career, from Kinston (1980-81) through Syracuse (1982-83). He played 15 games with the big club in the 1983 season.

Blue Jay chaplain David Fisher remembers Tony's tension:

"Tony came to me in Syracuse one Sunday after a chapel, and I could tell he really wanted to commit his life to Christ. But he also knew he had this 'superstar' or 'can't miss' label on him. He didn't know if becoming a Christian would make him less of a success as a ball player. He didn't know if it would cramp his style. He knew he should commit his life to Christ but he just didn't know how he would handle it."

Fernandez came to the Blue Jays still torn by the inner dilemma. He admits that when things were going well, he ignored his deep-felt need to become a Christian, but when things went badly – such as the broken wrist he suffered in Syracuse – he'd call on God for help. But he'd forget about God as soon as his circumstances took a turn for the better.

Finally he realized that he didn't have the resources within himself to go on alone, without God. The man who's now becoming a superstar saw his game in decline, and instead of calling on God for temporary, instant aid, as he had in the past, he made a complete commitment of his life to Jesus Christ.

Fisher remembers that it made all the difference in Tony. The man with all the skills to be a star suddenly found the confidence that supplied a concrete base for the full development of his potential. The chaplain says, "Tony wasn't sure of himself. But when he did commit his life to Christ, that confidence and maturity emerged. He suddenly realized that he could be a vibrant Christian and a successful ballplayer, and that he didn't need to allow the success to go to his head and jeopardize

58

his Christian life."

"He's really mature. He's only about two years old as a believer – it was June 1984 – but he really means business. And he's a great ballplayer."

It probably will come as no surprise that Tony credits the Blue Jays' spiritual leader, Roy Lee Jackson, and Jesse Barfield with influencing him to return to his roots of faith. Perhaps Tony saw in these men that it was possible to be a faithful believer and a good ballplayer. He states: "Roy Lee Jackson and Jesse Barfield were the two responsible for my being a born-again Christian today. Jesse was always witnessing to me about Jesus, but I always told him that my chance would come, that I was still young, but some day I'd accept Christ Jesus. But he still insisted on talking about how I needed Jesus Christ in my life."

Tony considers Barfield's efforts to have been anything but high-pressure. Instead, he credits his friend and teammate with telling him the truth that he needed to accept.

"Thanks to God that I came back in time. If I were to die without Christ in my heart, it would be over for me. I came back to Him and He helped me. And I can tell you one thing: I have the peace that I was looking for, right now, in Christ Jesus."

Of all of the Blue Jays who claim the designation "born again," Tony is perhaps the most consistently outspoken. Whether discussing fielding, hitting or finances, Tony naturally and automatically brings God into the conversation. He admits that being as outspoken as he is can bring ridicule at times, but he shrugs it off.

"I get laughed at or criticized once in a while, but I don't care. I have Jesus and that's what counts for me. As long as I have Jesus in my heart, and as long as I'm happy, I don't care what anybody says. I'm just trying to please God; that's the main thing for me. Baseball is my job, and I know that I have to take care of my job. But people don't understand that this thing is going to pass away one day, so I have to still look for those eternal things that are going to last forever, like spiritual life."

That is not to suggest that Fernandez gives anything but his best as a ballplayer. John Robertson has implied in *The Sun* that Tony's newly found focus for his life has made him a more determined major leaguer: "He plays the game as he lives his life. With quiet dignity. With total dedication."

Tony might be embarrassed by the praise, but he also believes that his faith has improved his performance on the diamond. "Before, I used to worry a lot about certain things on the field. I'm still working on it. But every time I'm going through some bad stretch, I just put everything in God's hands, and I know things are going to work out for the best. I say always in my heart, 'All things work together for good to those who love God.'

"And being a born-again Christian can only help me in my game. I play harder, because I know who I'm playing for. If I'm a Christian and I'm playing for the glory of God, I don't want to let the Christian life be a shame in the eyes of the people. I don't want to let Christ down. I want to lift Him up and do the best so that His name can be glorified through me in this world, in the job that I do."

Like Barfield and Moseby, Fernandez doesn't believe God has given him additional skills in his chosen profession. But he does fervently insist that he's a better player because he's a Christian. The slim, thoughtful infielder points to several examples:

"There've been so many good moments – as well as bad moments – in my career. I think one of the best moments for me was when I won this job. I was praying the whole way into it, asking the Lord for a starting job somewhere, and finally it came true."

The Jays had to shuffle personnel to open up the permanent place on the diamond for their young shortstop. Long-time Jay Alfredo Griffin, a compatriot of Fernandez, was traded to Oakland with Dave Collins. The Jays obtained relief pitcher Bill Caudill in the deal and were able to move Tony off the bench and into the batting order. Tony and Alfredo have remained good friends despite the competition for one position and are off-season neighbours in the Dominican Republic.

Tony continues, thoughtfully: "I remember when the team was in Milwaukee and I was in a bad stretch. My batting average had come down to .271 and was still dropping, and I just prayed to God: 'Lord, this is in your hands. I know that you're not going to let me down. It's almost the end of the season.'

"That day, after I put God on top of everything, I went four for five, and my batting average started going up again."

Did God give him the base hits? Tony doesn't believe it's that simple. Instead, he says, "I put Him ahead of everything and I said, 'It doesn't matter what happens; You're still going to be my Lord and my King, You're still going to be Lord of my life, and You're going to be on top, always, in my life. Having that confidence in God and putting all my trust in Him helps me a lot in my life and in my game."

Then Fernandez turns the focus away from himself, as he does consistently, and urges other people to discover the same truths he has found. "I know it will help anybody's game. And more than a game, it will help anyone, wherever you are, if you put God first, if you put your trust in God."

Tony believes that family relationships are bound to benefit from a commitment to Christ. He's been married to his wife, Clara, for two years, and they have one son who, like the children of many of the Blue Jay believers, bears a Biblical name: Joel.

He declares that his ultimate relationship is with Jesus, but Tony isn't a Lone Ranger in his faith. He credits his friendship with other Christians on the team with helping him to grow spiritually. And the growing number of believers on the team has sparked even greater enthusiasm in chapel services and informal time spent together.

Tony says, "Having a strong group of Christians on this team helps a lot, because we get together and study the word of God more often. It's tougher when there are only a few in there, but when you have more and more guys, you're more pleased. The more there are on the club, the better it is for you to grow."

But because the believers become so close, it's much harder when one of them leaves, either traded to another club or cut from the squad.

David Fisher recalls Roy Lee Jackson's release with intense emotion.

"I remember the day he was cut in spring training, in 1985. It was a very sad day for the team. All the Christians were upset. Tony and I sat on a tarpaulin behind the clubhouse and cried together.

"There's still a great deal of respect for Roy Lee. In October 1985 on the final Sunday, we had a celebration chapel, because they had clinched the American League East. When it was Lloyd Moseby's turn to share in that service, he said, 'There's one man I'd like to pay tribute to. I think a lot of our success this year – a lot of my success, at least – is because of Roy Lee Jackson.' "

Some believe that Jackson had fallen into disfavour with the Blue Jays because of his outspoken testimony to his faith in Christ. Whether or not Tony Fernandez shares that opinion, it certainly hasn't deterred him from following in the footsteps of his mentor.

He is open with his comments to the news media and the fans, and he also speaks freely about his faith in the off-season, when he's at home in the Dominican Republic. Major League baseball players are even bigger superstars in that island nation than they are in the United States and Canada – almost every boy at some time decides he will escape the impoverished life-style by using bat and ball, and those who've actually accomplished that are gigantic heroes.

But it's almost unheard of for a major leaguer to return home as a born-again Christian. Tony's an exception, and he knows it.

He says, "Here in Canada it's nothing new that an athlete becomes a born-again Christian, but in the Dominican it is. So when an athlete becomes born again, everyone's surprised, and everyone's talking about him. Some people say I'm crazy! Why would I become a born-again Christian when I have my whole future ahead of me? They just don't know what the Christian life is all about, so I explain it to them."

He accepts any opportunity he can to give that explanation. "When I get the chance, I go to the church and testify. I also speak to the people and to the press. I always give my testimony, getting up in any place. I don't feel ashamed of God, because the gospel is the power of God. So every time I get a chance to testify, I take it. I feel like I'm growing more and more, and I'm getting more confidence."

He also enthusiastically encourages his Dominican friends to read Christian books. The Blue Jays' information guide notes that Tony's favourite hobby is reading – but it doesn't mention that he reads almost nothing but Christian literature. He says, "I've been reading a lot of books. I try to read as much as I can, because as you read you get spiritually stronger and stronger, and you grow. You must read the Word of God, because He speaks to us through His Word. If you don't read, if you don't study His Word, how are you going to grow?"

Most of his reading is in Spanish, although Tony's English – reading and speaking – has improved dramatically. He does read English books supplied by Jesse Barfield's pastor in Texas, books concerning miracles and divine healing.

Has his eager missionary activity made any difference in his homeland? Tony believes it has, with God's help: "I think that a lot of people are getting ready and are just about to give their lives to Christ Jesus." For Fernandez, that would be better than hitting .350 and having no errors in a season.

That's not to suggest that hitting and throwing are no longer important in his life. He worked hard in spring training to add accuracy to his first base throws. Throughout the spring and into the early 1986 season Tony was hampered with an extremely sore foot. In the early days of training camp in Dunedin Florida, his foot would be so tender after practice that he could only hobble around the dressing room.

But that didn't stop him from taking an active part in the workouts and practice drills, and he eagerly took the field for the spring training games as soon as the coaching staff allowed him to. He's determined to have a better season in 1986, which might be tough to do considering his 1985 statistics.

First priority is cutting down on errors. In 1985 he made 30 errors in 791 chances, for a respectable .962 fielding average. But for Tony, 30 is too many. He says, "I just want my arm to get better so I can make fewer throwing errors. Maybe I can make under 20 this year."

But his conversation doesn't stay with fielding percentages for very long. He states his most important goal: "I'm trying just to please God any way I can, and to be patient on and off the field, so He can show His love through me. I just ask God to shine through me, because we're the light of the world, so I want to let Jesus Christ take over for me."

The shortstop who left the Dominican Republic determined that Tony Fernandez would be "someone" has undergone a marked change in priorities: "I don't want to be just Tony Fernandez. I want to be Tony Fernandez, the born-again Christian who puts everything in God's hands, who trusts God. I want to show that I'm a Christian. I want to show that I care more about Christ than I care about anything else in the world. That's my goal this year – I want to put Christ first. I don't care what anybody says; I'm glad to be a born-again Christian. I'm more than happy!"

Chapter 5

Willie Upshaw

He's the quiet man. He's solid, steady, and shy. Even the most dedicated Blue Jays fans know very little about Willie Clay Upshaw, except that he's a consistent first baseman, a good left-handed hitter, he wears number 26 on his back, and that his name must be the favourite of the Blue Jays' public address system announcer, who simply loves to announce that the next batter is: "Wil-lie UPPP-shaw!!!"

But those who know Willie Upshaw on a more personal level have nothing but good to say about the Jays' infield anchorman.

Broadcaster Jerry Haworth notes the apparent contradiction between Willie's shyness and his authority as he relates to his teammates: "Willie is probably the quietest leader on the ball club." He sees Upshaw's quiet nature as the product of self-confidence, not simple shyness. "He just exudes respect and confidence. He's a family man."

Unlike many of the young Blue Jays, Willie, who turned 29 on April 27, 1986, is no newlywed. He and Cindy have been married for several years, and they share their permanent home in Fairfield, Connecticut, with their three children – Brock Anthony, Courtney and Chad.

Haworth says that Upshaw's fellow Blue Jays know that Willie is a fine adviser and teacher; they frequently come to him for advice, because they know he takes his job seriously and that he plays and practises with great dedication.

The radio commentator says with respect that, "Willie goes about his business on the baseball field like a businessman. He's a professional, he works hard and he sets a good example. But he never goes to anybody and says, 'Here's how you should do it.' Those people eventually come to Willie and say, 'How can I do it?' and Willie says, 'Well, if you want my opinion, I'll give it to you.'

"In his own quiet, easy-mannered way Willie sets the tenor of this ball club. It's not an outgoing club, and it's not a raucous ball club. They're quietly confident that they can go about their business and win a lot of ball games."

It's certainly true that the Blue Jays are apparently more low-key than many other ball clubs. Haworth may well be right in attributing the mellow and relaxed clubhouse atmosphere at least partly to the respected anchorman, Willie Upshaw.

That doesn't mean there are never any high jinks in the locker room. You've already read Lloyd Moseby's confession about the not-so-mysterious pre-game disappearances of gloves and shoes that bear the Upshaw monogram. It also isn't rare in the clubhouse for other practical jokes to be perpetrated. During spring training, catcher Ernie Whitt arrived at his locker one morning to find every piece of equipment, every article of clothing, and everything else in the locker carefully and thoroughly taped together.

Ernie had two responses. First he calmly asked manager Jimy Williams for permission to be a bit late for practice; and then he threatened the bodily well-being of the members of the Blue Jays staff whom he suspected of guilt.

Of course, Whitt had shared responsibility for the prank in a previous season when one of the training staff was discovered by fans sleeping in a ball park where the Jays were visiting the club. The staffer was taped, mummy-fashion, from head to foot, and had been dumped in the bleachers. Whitt wasn't alone in that effort, and most eyes looked toward perpetual practical joker Bill Caudill as another likely culprit.

Humour and practical jokes are an important part of the baseball world. They serve a valuable role in reducing the tensions in a multi-million dollar industry that rests on the abilities of men to hit a ball with a stick or catch a ball someone else has hit with his stick. Every player on the team has at least one nickname – Upshaw is known as "Chuckie," for no apparent reason, or "Wilson" as a play on his name – and friendly insults fly like pollen in the springtime. A consistent theme in the Blue Jays clubhouse has to do with Cliff Johnson's hefty frame and rugged visage – usually interpreted by his teammates as "ugly." One would be wise to make that observation a safe distance from Heathcliff.

During a batting practice, Lloyd Moseby was heading for the batting cage, bat in hand, when a female fan began to plead with him to come over and sign her autograph book.

Unfortunately, she was addressing Lloyd as "Willie," acting on the mistaken impression that he was the first baseman. Lloyd turned to her with a long look of amazement and then went to the cage where he voiced his complaint to batting coach Cito Gaston.

"Willie!" harrumphed Lloyd.

"Relax," said Cito, laconically. "She might have called you Cliff."

"I would have had to hit her," was Moseby's quick response.

Their fellow players are not the only victims of jests. Most of the Blue Jays are willing to spend a lot of time with the fans, talking, having their pictures taken, and signing their names over and over again. Like almost all of his teammates, second baseman Damaso Garcia is willing to spend time along the fences of the ballparks, autographing books, slips of paper, programs, balls, hats and occasionally forearms and foreheads. But some of the eager fans might well arrive home to find that their book or baseball reads "Wade Boggs," "Dave Winfield," "Gary Carter," or any other major league name that popped into Garcia's mind.

The pranks and high spirits on the Jays, from all reports, seem to rate a description that almost sounds old-fashioned in this day of cocaine and all manner of other pursuits and addictions: they just have good, relatively clean fun.

Maybe Upshaw does have something to do with that atmosphere. He's a veteran of the Blue Jays team, having played in a Jays' uniform in 1978 and from 1980 on. In 1978 he came up to the Blue Jays and played his first big-league game as an outfielder, something his buddies Moseby and Barfield might find a trifle amusing. Of course, he could point out to Lloyd that he was never required to take diving practice.

His first major league home run, smacked that year, was from star reliever Goose Gossage. Since that occasion, Upshaw has frequently thrown a wet blanket on noted "firemen" – pitchers coming in from the bullpen to relieve a beleagured starter. When he was recalled from Syracuse in 1980, Upshaw again faced Gossage, and this time snapped the Goose's 29-consecutive-batter hitless streak with a pinch-hit single. In 1981 Upshaw swatted the Blue Jays' only pinch-hit home run of the entire season from – you guessed it – Goose Gossage.

Upshaw inherited the full-time position of first baseman in 1982, after John Mayberry was traded to the Yankees. No doubt Yankee Goose Gossage would have preferred that Willie be traded to somewhere safe – like to Goose's own team, where Gossage would never have to face him when it counted.

Willie's professional career stretches back to 1975, when he actually began the upward climb in the New York Yankees' farm system. Before he got close to a major league Yankee uniform and the notorious owner, George Steinbrenner – or to Gossage – he was picked by the Toronto Blue Jays in the major league draft in December 1977.

Willie's an expert at keeping the peace in a rowdy setting – like a baseball locker room – perhaps because he happens to be one of 15 children born to the Upshaw household in Blanco, Texas, where his parents still live. His mom and dad attend the games every time Willie and the Jays play the Texas Rangers in Arlington. The size of his family may also explain his taciturn nature: it may be that he simply never got an opportunity to make an extended speech.

Those speculations, if they happen to be true,

aren't the only impact his family had on Willie. He began playing organized baseball in Texas, when he was seven years old, and he says he can never remember any other goal in life than to play baseball in the big leagues. But he really set his sights on a career as a professional athlete when he first saw his cousins playing college football on their way to professional careers. Those cousins are National Football League greats Gene and Marvin Upshaw.

The excitement and challenge of professional sport reached out and grabbed Willie when he saw Gene and Marvin play. He was only ten years old. But though he was young, he insists, "That's when I realized I wanted to be a professional athlete, especially once they got into the pros."

It took six and a half years in the minors, with brief visits to the big club, before Willie realized his dream of playing major league ball. Perhaps he wished at times he'd followed his cousins onto the football field but, while he stands six feet tall and weighs 185 pounds, he might have been too small for that particular big man's game.

But in a Blue Jays uniform he's not small in any way – not when stretching his game glove high into the air or in the dirt along the baseline to snare an off-line throw to first, nor when powering the 88 home runs he'd hit his major league career by the end of the 1985 season. He smacked 27 of those in 1983, his most productive long-ball year. Also in 1983, Willie set the Blue Jays' record for most runs batted in, with 104, nine ahead of George Bell's second-place 1985 total.

"The first three years (in the minors) were tough, but baseball has really been fun since I started," says Willie. "It's always been fun, but it seems the more I play it, the more I love it."

Upshaw was one of the Jays who seemed to be under-achieving in 1985, like Lloyd Moseby, but both men, who are close friends, have started the 1986 campaign with a bang. That's certainly part of Upshaw's game plan. Reflecting on 1985, he says,

"I had a good second half. I was hitting about .217, and I came up to .275 with a lot of at-bats and that's tough to do." In fact, to do it, he had to hit .351 after the all-star break, an astonishing improvement in home plate performance. To put that second-half achievement into perspective, you might realize that Boston's Wade Boggs, the American League batting champ, hit .368 on the season; second-place George Brett registered .335.

Even during his first-half slump in '85, Upshaw was not completely silent with the bat. His two home runs led the Jays to a win over Texas (with his parents in the stands in Arlington), and he contributed other game-winning blows.

Willie gives a quick overview of his plans for 1986: "This year, I want to be consistent for the whole year and not just for half the season."

It might be a boost to Willie's confidence in 1986 to know that he seems to have sewn up the job as first baseman. In '85 he played most of the games to the left of the pitching mound, but was spelled on occasion by new Jay Cecil Fielder. This year Fielder is still around on occasion, but the second-year man is apparently contending for the spot as designated hitter (usually held by big Cliff Johnson), not for first base. Willie can relax – he's again a permanent fixture.

About that apparent competition Willie says, "Well, I just tried to put it in perspective. I had confidence in myself that I was going to do well. You need confidence in order to play. I didn't feel that the competition was any threat because I have confidence in my ability. That's just the way I try to go about it."

He admits he's set extremely high goals for himself in the current campaign. His objectives show that his quietness indeed covers a real personal confidence:

"I always have goals. I set them very high. They're probably not attainable, but I know that if I get close I'm going to be very respectable."

The numbers for '86? "In the 20-25 range in home runs" – he hit 15 in '85. "I'd like to drive in 100 runs" – he had 65 RBIs in 1985. "Hit .300 again" – something he accomplished in 1983, when he shared Most Valuable Player honours with Lloyd Moseby; but in 1985 he slumped in the first months of the season, then powered his way back to a .275 average.

It is completely foreign to Willie Upshaw's nature to brag about his achievements. When asked about the highlights of his career, he simply says, "I don't really think about it a lot." When pressed for an answer, he smiles briefly and – almost as though he is making a confession – says, "I've had some good days. The day I knocked in my 100th and 101st RBIs, the first Blue Jay to do that (on September 20, 1983). The day I hit two home runs. . ., and the next day I hit two more. Four home runs in two days, that was a great feeling."

He sounds almost embarrassed to admit his accomplishments, even though they're easy to find in the record book.

He's certainly soft-spoken and confesses that he's always been shy. Perhaps that's why Roy Lee Jackson didn't instantly spot Willie as a fellow believer when Jackson came to the Jays from the Mets. But as other Blue Jays, beginning with Moseby and Barfield, came to confess faith in Christ, they discovered they had a "brother" playing first base – a brother who was absolutely delighted to find a growing number of fellow Christians on the team roster.

Willie leaves no doubt that he's one of the born-again Blue Jays. When asked a carefully ambiguous question like, "What does it mean to you to be a Christian?" Willie's response is clear and straightforward:

"Well, I know that the Lord Jesus Christ is my Saviour, and that He died for me. Right now, I just want to do His will on earth, to be as Christ-like as possible. I want to try to do things here on earth that will prepare myself for the after-life in heaven."

That's about as direct a baseball player's catechism as you could find. And yet, Willie isn't as widely known to be a Christian as some of the other Blue Jays stars. That's probably due to personality, not level of spirituality. Willie himself admits, "I've always been a shy person, and I don't have to be flamboyant to be me. But I know what I can do, and I know that all the strength that I get and everything that I do comes from the Lord."

David Fisher, who spends as much time as possible listening to and sharing with the individual Jays, says that Upshaw "is a strong Christian. I think Willie has a very deep-rooted belief in God and in Jesus Christ – I really sense that when he talks to me."

Willie also spends a lot of time with Lloyd Moseby, with whom he shares the very biblical love of fishing. When Willie's not fishing in the off-season, he can be found – surprise!! – playing sports. Now that's a sure sign of a genuine, in-love-with-sports athletic nut.

His spiritual roots are deep. They began to flourish almost half his lifetime ago in Blanco, Texas. He says, "I was baptized in a Baptist church when I was about 17. I've been with the Lord a long time. I know that a few years after high school, in minor league ball, I wasn't really into the Lord like I was supposed to be."

That's another thing about Willie – his humble honesty. He may not say at lot, but when he does, the odds are 100 percent that it's going to be the truth. He openly admits that he had a time when he was failing as a Christian.

"I guess I was sitting on that fence again, because of my being out in the world by myself for the first time. I was something of a follower for a while, and then I got back to being strong in my faith like I was when I was younger and when I had guidance from my parents."

Willie is very happy that other believers share the benches at the clubhouse lockers. His friends on the team sometimes play the same role his family did back home in Texas – they provide the guidance and the support to keep one another on track in their faith. Upshaw says, "It helps tremendously because it gives you someone to have fellowship with day in and day out. It's tough to do it on your own."

The quiet first baseman has always seemed to be a rock on the corner of the diamond. His consistency at first has never been in question, and he had only ten errors in 1271 plays at first in 1985. He claims that his faith in Christ contributes to that stability.

"Actually, it helps to be a ball player and a Christian. Once you go out there on the field, it just seems that it's a lot easier. Things don't bother me as much as they would if I didn't know I was saved and that there would be a tomorrow."

He says that his favourite verse of Scripture – although a lot of biblical passages are important to him – is the tough message written by the Apostle Paul: "For all have sinned and come short of the glory of God" (Romans 3:23). That statement on its own could be downright depressing, but the next verse provides the answer: we can be redeemed, or rescued, through Christ Jesus.

The verse is important to Willie because it's a direct reminder about the true nature of "glory." Baseball players, especially those on a team that won the American League East pennant, come in for a lot of glory. Willie needs only to read that verse to remind himself that whatever fame, honour or glory might come his way, those honours have no worth at all in God's eternal value system.

That's how Upshaw stays humble – and everyone who knows him will confirm that not even fame found the right nozzle to inflate Willie's ego.

Upshaw's friendship with the other believers on the team has helped to encourage him to be more outspoken about his faith, although his personality will never allow him to be exactly like Lloyd Moseby or Tony Fernandez. He believes that his friendships with those men and the others involved in chapel and in Bible studies, has really contributed to personal growth in his own life.

Willie says, "The fellowship with these guys on the club is really important to my growth. I think I've grown spiritually more in the last three years than I ever have before."

Perhaps one mark of that development can be seen by what happens when the Blue Jays come into a new city for a game. Some of the players might head for a favourite bar for a few quick ones, but following the Moseby-Barfield-Upshaw trio would leave you with a dry throat.

Willie confesses: "We go to Christian bookstores in almost every city we're in, Lloyd, Jesse and myself."

And while some of the guys might be listening to rock tapes or classical music on the plane, that's not what's playing into the Upshaw headphones. "In my spare time, while we're on the plane or bus, I listen to study tapes or I just try to sit down and read the word of the Lord. That's how I relax."

So the next time you see number 26, Willie UPP-shaw, playing first base in his usual relaxed, steady, consistent manner – you'll know why!

Chapter 6

Mark Eichhorn

"Hey, you!"

I looked up to see a tall, hefty guy wearing number 38 on his Blue Jays' uniform.

"I hear that you're interviewing the Christians on this team."

"That's right," I answered.

"So how come you haven't talked to me?"

This first conversation I had with Mark Eichhorn is a wonderful example of the eagerness of the Blue Jay believers to share their faith in Jesus Christ.

The truth was, I had been told that a non-roster pitcher named Mark Eichhorn was a believer, and some of the younger players at training camp had told me to talk with him. But I'd decided not to do so – as a dedicated Blue Jays fan, I knew that the guy had already had an opportunity to play with the Jays a few years back, and had turned in a mediocre performance. After only 35 days in the major leagues, Eichhorn had been sent back to the minors, and had remained there ever since.

With the number of up-and-coming pitchers in the camp, I reasoned that Mark had little or no chance of making the team, and since everyone else

I was interviewing was on the forty-man roster, I decided not to find time for him in a very busy interviewing schedule. . . . All of which only proves how wrong this writer can be.

After that direct confrontation, initiated by the tall right-hander, I found the time for a conversation. The subsequent developments in the early '86 season have demonstrated that Mark had every right to expect to be included in a book about believers on the Blue Jays squad; because when the Blue Jays' season opened on April 8 in Texas, "Ike" was there, all six feet, three inches and 200 pounds of him.

Mark Eichhorn (pronounced Ike-Horn) has to be listed near the top of pleasant Blue Jay surprises in 1986. His professional baseball career has been spent touring the minor leagues, ever since he left his home in San Jose, California, at the age of 18. He has played in Medicine Hat (1979), Kinston (1980), Knoxville (1981, 1983, 1985) and Syracuse (1982, 1983, 1984, 1985). His pitching record has never been of "superstar" quality, although his performance in 1982 caught the eye of the Blue Jays brass.

His shot at the major leagues came when the Blue Jays called him up at the end of August to replace injured Jim Gott. While he remained in the Blue Jays uniform for the rest of the season, his performance was unimpressive – he won no games, lost three, and had a relatively high earned run average of 5.45 (5.45 earned runs scored for every nine innings pitched). He appeared in seven games, walked almost as many batters as he struck out (14 walks, 16 strike-outs), and threw three wild pitches over that short span, all of which was enough to guarantee a return trip to the minors for the 1983 season.

He came to spring training in 1986 knowing it was probably his last chance to earn a place on the Blue Jays major league squad. And the odds didn't look good in a training camp packed with pitchers, many of whom were returning after fine seasons with the Blue Jays in 1985 – Dave Steib, Jimmy Key, Jim Clancy, Doyle Alexander, Jim Acker, Tom Henke, Dennis Lamp, Gary Lavelle and Bill Caudill – good pitchers who had served the club well in the drive to the pennant. That list left one possible opening on the team, and there were at least nine hurlers competing for that one apparent spot.

But Eichhorn loves throwing baseballs, and he accepted the challenge. After his dismal showing in 1982, he had returned to the minors to completely rethink his approach to pitching. When he last wore the Blue Jays uniform, he was a powerful overhand fastball pitcher with severe control problems. He came back in 1986 with a whole new style – a sidearm delivery that is almost submarine style – which somehow retained his power but added the crucial element of control. His new approach, similar to that of ace Kansas City reliever Dan Quisenberry, had been suggested by Blue Jay pitching coach Al Widmar and bullpen coach John Sullivan.

Eichhorn admits that he took their advice out of desperation, spurred by an almost total lack of effectiveness in his pitching, but the improvement in his performance earned him the invitation to spring training in Dunedin as a non-roster player.

Injuries to Blue Jays pitchers opened the door a crack for Mark Eichhorn, along with two other relative newcomers, Don Gordon and Steve Davis. Despite being what sportswriter John Robertson accurately described as "a rank outsider at the start of training camp," Mark was with the club at the start of 1986 as the tenth pitcher on a ten-man pitching squad. His early season efforts have sparkled, and Mark may have found a place in the major leagues at last. Blue Jays coaches have happily conceded that Eichhorn has become a major league pitcher.

His initial 1986 efforts left him with a better earned run average than he's ever registered in the minor leagues, and he gained his first-ever major league win in a tense battle with the Texas Rangers that the struggling Jays needed, on April 21. In an understatement uncharacteristic of Mark Eichhorn, he termed the win "very satisfying."

If things continue to break toward Eichhorn's way, his may be the premier success story of the 1986 Blue Jays. He may be forging one of the most impressive come-backs in recent memory.

As the saying goes, it couldn't happen to a nicer guy. Mark Eichhorn seems to bubble with humour. He's likely to reduce a group of friends to laughing fits with wondrous impersonations and strange, frenetic dance steps. His humour is probably what's kept the 25-year-old bachelor going through all those seasons of undistinguished baseball. He can generally see the positive side to almost any situation, and no one could stay depressed around him for very long.

He can even find a positive perspective on his terrible 1982 fling with major league baseball, although in this case his optimism has a serious tone. It was during that stint with the Jays that he became a born-again Christian.

Once again the key people were Roy Lee Jackson and Jesse Barfield. In this case it may be even more significant than it was for Lloyd Moseby or Tony Fernandez, because Jackson and Barfield are black, and Eichhorn is white. Even in modern-day baseball, with the colour barrier long broken and Jackie Robinson a legendary name from the past, racial distinctions still exist on ball clubs.

They may not be expressed in overt, racist terms, but it is soon obvious that the white players tend to associate most with whites, and the black players with blacks. Yet in this case, Jackson, Barfield and Eichhorn were relaxing and talking together. That situation is not at all rare with believers on baseball teams; their shared faith seems to crumble any vestiges of racial prejudice.

Mark recalls the occasion: "It was in 1982, when I was in the big leagues, at a game in Seattle. We were up in the hotel room, and I'd been talking with Jesse Barfield and Roy Lee Jackson a lot during the season.

"I had always gone to church, and I'd been a 'good guy,' but I'd never really accepted Jesus into my life until that time."

Eichhorn had discovered that being a "good guy" and attending church really didn't meet the need he felt deep within, the same "void" that drew Moseby and Barfield to the Bible study at the Jackson apartment.

Mark explains, "I didn't feel that I had the peace. There was something missing, like inner strength, something I could really rely on. I went to church and I was a good guy, but I didn't feel the peace inside.

"Outwardly I might have looked like I was a real strong Christian, but I didn't have that peace."

His commitment to Christ n 1982 changed all that, at least for a while. But Eichhorn is honest enough to admit that at times he's failed to live the Christian life since then.

"It's been an up-and-down walk. It's been a struggle. It hasn't been roses, to be honest. I've been battling like I'm sure most Christians do with the everyday temptations."

Most Christian leaders will suggest that this is very normal – Christians are involved in a spiritual battle against sin and temptation, and a young Christian is subject to the kind of spiritual attacks that Lloyd Moseby talked about.

Mark admits he didn't always handle those conflicts very well. He says, "I think I really strayed farthest from Christianity after I accepted Jesus. When I was sent down to the minors after pitching pretty well in Toronto in 1982, it was a big blow to me. I was the last player to be cut in spring training."

And then, during the 1983 season, Eichhorn encountered conflicts with the manager of his minor league club. Mark says, "He and I didn't hit it off too well, and I didn't rely on Jesus – I went the other way. And I really struggled. I lost my poise on and off the field. I think that was the time when I really strayed away from Jesus."

"I started drinking, I started partying, and I really didn't rely on what Jesus says; I didn't have faith in Him. Things just piled up, and I wasn't taking each day at a time with Him. I didn't allow Him to work in my life."

But the six-foot-three-inch pitcher's face absolutely lights up when he makes the next statement: "But you can always come back."

There's real joy on his face – probably more than he felt after his initial major league win against Texas – as Mark declares, "He's always there for you. That's my main goal this year – not only to have a good season (he's well on the way), but to be as good a Christian as I can off the field, and to use my time off the field as well as I possibly can. It might be to help kids or to do something constructive that will glorify Jesus. I believe that I do have the Holy Spirit within me, and I just need to nurture it."

His efforts to grow have centred on a consistent pattern of Bible reading. Mark says, "I think that for me the most important thing is to stay in the Word. When I wake up each morning, I need to offer my day up to God then and there, and to do my Bible studying then, so I can meditate on it later.

"Otherwise, some days I'll get right up and, Boom! I'll be right into the daily rush routine. But if I do that, I miss the whole point of living."

Eichhorn has completely changed his approach to pitching, and his new style seems to have brought him success for the first time in a hard-fought professional baseball career. He also has altered his approach to life – and his new focus on obedience and commitment to Jesus Christ is giving him the peace and joy in living that a successfully submarined fastball could never bring.

Chapter 7

Kelly Gruber

The blonde third baseman moves a step or two deeper and eases to the left, trying to be ready for anything the next batter may try to blast past him. His face is intent, his prominent jaw locked in concentration. This man is serious about baseball and even more serious about becoming an integral part of the Toronto Blue Jays squad. In 1984 he played a mere 15 games in the Blue Jay uniform, hitting only .063 in 16 at bats (that represents exactly one hit, which happened to be a home run). In 1985 his hitting improved to .231, but his at-bats decreased to 13 in a brief Blue Jays stint. His three hits were all singles.

Those days of fly-in visits to Toronto and occasional, inconsequential insertions into the line-up should now be in the past.

You can tell from the determination in his eyes that he's serious. You can tell from the set of his jaw; you can tell by the slightly crouched, ready-to-spring stance. You can tell from the great pink bubble that emerges from his lips . . . well, maybe not. His excellent, large bubbles, produced from the chunks of Bazooka gum ever-available in the clubhouse, may show another side of this new Jay.

In total, these vignettes provide a good picture of Kelly Gruber. He's intensely dedicated to the game of baseball and completely determined to forge a place for himself on the Toronto Blue Jays. He simply believes he *should* be on the team, for the good of the Jays and the good of Kelly Gruber. But just when this intense young man seems to be carried away by his determination, under that ambitious exterior he gives you a glimpse of a happy and peaceful person. Outside, he's always sliding hard, head first, into second base. Inside, he's happily blowing pink bubble-gum bubbles – and never popping them in a sticky accident onto that prominent, Brian Mulroney jaw.

Kelly thinks he should have been a permanent member of the Blue Jays in 1985. The team was saddled with an obligation to carry two minor league ballplayers on the major league roster – Manny Lee and Lou Thornton – for the entire season, or they would have lost them through the intricacies of major league drafting procedures. Both men have been assigned to the minors for the 1986 season. But the necessity of having Lee and Thornton on the 25-man roster (unofficially reduced to 24 for '86) left considerably less room for an up-and-comer like Kelly Gruber (as well as several others who might have added to the Jays' bench strength), and although Kelly did play five games with the Jays in the winning afternoons of the season, he spent his year in Syracuse.

When he came up to the big club in September, he arrived bearing no apparent malice over his rejection in the spring, and instead filled in when required, giving his best. He played in only five games, but in one of them – September 21 – he smacked the game-winning single in the 14th inning of a tight pitchers' battle to beat Milwaukee 2-1. That effort chalked up a crucial Blue Jays victory in the tense pennant race in the American League East.

Like the other "junior Jays," he left the club at the end of the regular season and had no part in the play-off battles. But while other Jays who caught an early plane home were complaining that they felt left out of the excitement, Gruber was telling reporters that his plans involved a fitness program at his home in Austin Texas and a full-out effort in winter ball, so that he would come to spring training in 1986 ready to make the big club once and for all.

His dedication seems to have paid off. Kelly Gruber is now one of the reasons observers are crediting the Blue Jays with improved bench strength this season. The likes of Gruber, Rick Leach and Cecil Fielder have added depth to the club; and as the Jays struggled with injuries and occasional ineptitude in the early days of '86, especially on the part of some of their most noted pitchers, it was often Gruber and his benchmates who salvaged a game for the club. His statistical numbers for the spring training season sparkled in comparison to his previous visits to the club.

He's no longer a visitor. Kelly Wayne Gruber's uniform, number 17, should hang in the Blue Jays clubhouse throughout the entire season this time around – and maybe this year he'll still be wearing it during league championship and World Series games.

Spring training is often a reasonably relaxed time for players like Lloyd Moseby, Jesse Barfield or Willie Upshaw. They can come to camp almost certainly assured of their places on the Jays, and the weeks in Dunedin offer pleasurable moments for men who work out and play a little ball during the day and go home to their families – usually based in Florida – for the late afternoon and early evening hours. Many of the players see more of their wives and children during spring training than they do for the rest of the grueling, six-month season.

But there is very little ease for men like Kelly Gruber, men who are doing their very best and working their very hardest, to earn their way onto an already solid and stable squad. In the Florida days, Gruber did everything asked of him. He considers himself to be a third baseman, but he's played anywhere they've placed him – and they send him almost everywhere! During the weeks down south, Kelly played seven of the nine positions on the field! – third base, second and short, all three spots in the outfield and, in the bullpen, catcher for the pitchers who were warming up. He claims that this simply kept him loose and happy, and as he succeeded in filling the gaps at all of those spots, he was able to show the coaches and managers how useful he could be to the team.

They also sent him up to bat frequently, and frequently he smacked the ball out of the park or hit safely in key situations.

He was playing well but, maybe to keep him humble, there were moments designed to rob sleep from aspiring ball players. In an exhibition game against the Texas Rangers, Gruber smacked the ball hard to centre field – the deepest part of the ball park. The fans were roaring, but Kelly wasn't sure how far the ball had carried; he thought he might have stroked a double. As he rounded second, his

Most Valuable Player – Jesse Barfield

Jesse and Marla Barfield – marriage restored

Jesse may have the best arm of any outfielder

Lloyd Moseby – confidence on the base paths

Lloyd Moseby "A tremendous leader"

Lloyd is off to a great start in 1986

Lloyd Moseby, Roy Lee Jackson and Jesse Barfield

"Flipper" – star short stop Tony Fernandez

Tony's intensity brought him out of poverty to the big leagues

"Antonio"

Chaplain Dave Fisher

Willie Upshaw – the quiet man

Willie lets his performance and integrity speak for him.

"A leader in the club house"

Mark Eichhorn — The biggest surprise of '86.

Kelly Gruber – played seven positions to make the team

Don Gordon – The Jays' give him a second chance

Steve Davis – one of baseball's best prospects

Jeff Hearron – battles back from injury

Garry Lavelle – an All Star sidelined by pain

Ron Shepherd – waiting for his chance

cleats caught on something, and he took a classic header, landing in the dirt beyond the plate. He scrambled quickly back to second.

Meanwhile, centre fielder Bobby Jones, chasing the ball, had also had foot problems, tripped, and fell down in centre field, all of which was doubly amusing because Gruber had actually hit a home run. Kelly could have walked around the bases, and Jones need not have moved. Gruber completed the circuit of the bases and arrived back in the Jays' dugout to a response of congratulations and good-natured ribbing.

Such occurrences bring out the "bubble-gum" side of Gruber – he's able to laugh them off and get on with what he's doing, and doing well – playing baseball and hitting the ball hard and often. Well enough, hard enough and often enough to earn him a locker in the Blue Jays dressing room as the 1986 season opened.

The man who had only 108 days of major league service – most of them on the bench – should easily triple that figure by the end of 1986. As early season injuries to Damaso Garcia and a sore Tony Fernandez foot hobbled the Blue Jays' infield , the club's management may have been congratulating themselves on the foresight they showed in keeping Gruber on the roster. After only a few 1986 season games, Kelly had already played several positions on the field and contributed with his bat, leaving the records of his earlier mini-series in the dust of the statistical books.

During previous seasons, the man now known as "Goob" – which he isn't crazy about – and "Chin" – an obvious appellation, but one that he likes even less – may have despaired of making the

89

team, in fact, of making any major league squad. After a stand-out career in high school sports in his home town of Bellaire, Texas – where he played baseball, quarterbacked the football team and starred in track – Kelly was the first-round pick of the Cleveland Indians in the 1980 free agent draft. He was chosen tenth overall – considered by the Cleveland crowd to be the tenth best young player in the nation.

Something didn't mesh in the marriage of the Indians and the Texan. By late 1983 they were willing to give him up in the major league draft, and on December 5, 1983, the Blue Jays, who are becoming noted for shrewd dealings on such occasions, picked up Kelly Gruber.

His career had already taken him to minor league clubs in Batavia, Waterloo (in the midwestern United States), Chattanooga and Buffalo. He now learned that his next stop was Syracuse, where he played in 1984 and 1985, with brief sojourns with the big club based in Toronto.

Jerry Haworth believes that Gruber was fortunate to be picked up by the Toronto system. He says,

"I think the best thing to happen to him was that the Blue Jays drafted him and he got into a new organization. Cleveland signed him, but maybe they didn't work with him as much as the Blue Jays have, and he's blossomed into a player who has a lot of power. He's got great tools."

Then Haworth points to one of the greatest mechanical obstacles for any new major leaguer: "He's got to learn to be a little more patient and try to handle the breaking ball at the plate." Judging from his contributions in early '86, Kelly's a good student.

But did Kelly have to learn as well to handle the disappointments in '84 and '85 when, after getting a taste of the big leagues, he was subsequently relegated to Syracuse? Of course – and Haworth believes he handled himself extremely well.

"Off the field, there's not a finer kid. When you start to think about all the money in the major league game, and then about the young players at Triple A who can't get to either the money or the prestige of 'the show,' he handles it pretty well.

"He doesn't get down on himself; he doesn't give up. He continues to work hard. He knows he's close, but he sees how Rance Mulliniks had to go through the same thing, and Garth Iorg, and Moseby. So he knows he's in an organization where the example's already been set, and he's a good follower of examples."

Those names, at least those of Mulliniks and Iorg, are evidence of the unique challenge facing Gruber – he's trying to make a club that already has two fine third basemen who "platoon" at that position (Iorg bats right-handed, Mulliniks left). With that already impressive combination at third, it may be that Kelly's willingness to move around the diamond has earned him his spot on the bench.

Gruber's attitude was probably watched as closely as his skills during spring training. Blue Jays management was well aware of his skills; Jimy Williams said, "He's an athlete. He has above-average speed and his stats show he has above-average power."

But it's likely that his gutsy determination was a contributing factor to another of Williams' observations, stated before the opening day roster was drawn up: "He's the type of player that you'd like to have."

They have him. Kelly has played well for the Jays in the early going of '86. He's apparently accomplished his first goal for 1986: "I'd like to stay with the Jays."

Now he can work toward accomplishing his other ambitions. It's unlikely that you'd guess number two – it has nothing to do with home runs or stolen bases though he registered in both categories early in the year; it isn't related to fielding percentages or even playing every day.

Kelly says, "I'd like to find a wife, settle down, share my life."

Kelly Gruber is a good-looking guy. At six feet and 180 pounds, with blonde hair and a Burt Lancaster style of strong-jawed face, this 24-year old bachelor (born February 26, 1962) is watched with considerable interest by a significant number of young women.

Some have confessed that if Gruber is on the bench, their attention tends to wander from the activities on the actual diamond.

It is obvious that one of the presumed benefits of promotion to any major league baseball squad is free association with available women, especially for a single guy like Kelly. But Gruber has a strong personal moral code, and while he welcomes friendships, he believes that intimate needs – sexual and otherwise – should be met only within the context of marriage.

He reflects on the benefits of such a permanent relationship: "Being single is kind of lonely. I wish I had somebody I could talk to. I have teammates and friends, but it's just not the same as having somebody to live with, where you are one. You and your spouse become one when you're married."

Instead of feeling excited about the potential of a

bachelor life-style, Kelly sees it as a potential pitfall. He holds that view because he believes sex before marriage is wrong. And he has come to that belief because he's been a born-again Christian for more than two years and he accepts the moral code of the Bible.

Gruber knew about Christianity long before it became a vital part of his life. He remembers: "I grew up in a good Christian home. I rebelled against it and had some childhood problems, especially because I was forced to go to church."

Kelly is obviously a determined (some might say "stubborn") kind of guy, and it would be difficult to force him to do anything against his will. That kind of coercion turned him against organized religion.

He remembers the early Sunday mornings: "I was forced to go to one denomination for nine o'clock mass and then after that, at 10:30, to go to the Church of Christ. So I was kind of pushed, and I rebelled against it."

His rebellion lasted until about the same time that he was taken from Cleveland by the Blue Jays. It was then that he realized he'd been running from the truth, but everywhere he went – to all those minor league towns – he took the truth buried somewhere deep inside him.

It was no new discovery when he began to think about Christianity again. He says, "I had a good foundation. People implanted it into my heart, my system and my mind, or else I don't know how I would react today.

"But Christianity has come easy to me because of that fact. Just finding good churches, and keeping fed upon the Word has really helped. I've been a full, born-again Christian for two or three years."

When he says that Christianity came easy, Kelly isn't implying that his is a life without struggles. He was able to accept the truth about Jesus Christ as Saviour and Lord with little inner turmoil, but he admits that the Christian life is a demanding one – again, especially for a bachelor who would really love to have a woman in his life.

His honesty can sometimes be shocking, but Kelly – like the other men featured in this book – isn't interested in being canonized as an athletic saint. Instead, he, like the others, freely admits to being an imperfect, still-learning, often-struggling Christian, seeking to allow God to teach and to work through His children, ballplayers who may be very new to this life of faith.

Regarding sexual opportunities, Kelly says, "Of all my downfalls, I guess that would be my biggest problem – sex. I don't have problems with alcohol or drugs or anything like that, because I just get high on Christianity and on knowing Christ. But that sex problem is tough."

The new Blue Jay believes that the best immediate answer is to keep on working to please God: "It's good to try to be with your brothers, to try to stay around them and strengthen each other." The born-again guys in spring training camp often share accommodations, and they meet at least on a weekly basis for Bible study and prayer. Usually spouses also come, plus a player or two from the Philadelphia Phillies, who train a couple of miles south in Clearwater. At the first study of the spring season, held in a private home in Dunedin, four of the young Jay hopefuls attended – all of whom appeared on the starting roster at the opening of the regular season.

On that occasion, Kelly asked the others to pray

for him as well as for themselves, that they would be able to deal with the temptations to sin that inevitably come their way. Kelly later expressed the problem with humour: "Maybe I should ask God to make me blind when I go to the beach." Again, he's bluntly frank, but most of us fully understand what the young ballplayer is talking about.

The group also looked at passages in the Bible that would help them to follow Christ in these matters, and they talked about their mutual problems before praying together.

Gruber looks beyond the immediate struggle to what he believes to be God's best answer to sexual drives: "I've been praying for a wife for about a year and a half now, thinking 'now's the time.' Not only am I starting to get to where I want to be financially, as well as spiritually, but this world's coming to an end, and I have good reason to believe that it's a blessing to have a wife. So I've been praying for a wife." He expects God to answer, but is willing to wait for God's best answer to his prayer.

Obviously, the Texan believes that God is ready to play an active part in his life, his relationships and his career. He seems to see his whole life now in terms of his relationship with Jesus Christ.

Asked for his personal definition of Christianity, Kelly speaks in terms of living and life-style. He says, "It's walking close to the Lord. It's trying to follow the example that Jesus Christ set when He was down here on this earth. Seeing how He handled situations and walked through life, it's an inspiration to us to follow in His footsteps."

But Gruber has no illusions about following Christ's footsteps to an easy life in a "rose garden," cleared of trouble or hardship. He acknowledges that Jesus was "born to die – it wasn't coincidence that He was wrapped in pieces of cloth to be buried."

Christ's example of absolute selflessness is crucial to Kelly. He knows that he isn't even close to living like his Master, but that doesn't stop him from trying – anymore than a demotion to the minor leagues stopped him from attempting to come back to the big club. He says, "It's a big achievement even to try to follow Christ. We'll never be able to walk the way He did with God, because He was God. But it's just magnificent to take on the fruits that God gives, and to let other people see Christ in your walk. There are all different kinds of testimonies in your life – talking with people and living the Christian life in front of people."

He is deeply concerned that he'll be able to set a God-honouring example no matter what team he is on.

For Kelly, one way to honour God is to do his very best at the job for which God has given him skills. That's why he uses a mad, head-first slide on stolen base attempts. That's why he's willing to play wherever they put him. That's why he could leave the club in early October 1985, not to complain or nurse emotional wounds, but to work his way back onto the Blue Jays' 24-man roster in 1986.

His love for God and his affection for baseball and the Toronto Blue Jays are both reflected – and even intertwined – as he looks ahead through 1986.

He says he is looking forward "to winning this championship and having a good testimony."

But there's an additional benefit, one that's seldom mentioned even by the other Christian ballplayers. Perhaps it's because there's so much focus on the money earned by – or at least paid to – professional athletes, that most of them duck the issue. After all, there's probably little rational justification for some of the salaries paid to the top-ranked players.

Gruber admits that he's looking forward to increases in remuneration, but not only to pad a comfortable life-style. Instead, he says, somewhat surprisingly, "I hope I'll be able to do the things I wasn't able to do, financially, for the Lord." He says that "riches in heaven" are much more important than financial success today, and he's eager to offer financial support to Christian ministries, especially an outreach to imprisoned convicts named "The Voice of Triumph Ministries," based in Bowden, West Virginia.

Kelly has a special affection for this group because his father is very involved in it as well. The Blue Jay passes out copies of a book entitled *I'm Gonna Bury You*, written by "Voice of Triumph" founder, Gene Neill.

The book finishes with a biblical quote that might well describe the goals of Blue Jay Kelly Gruber:

"Forgetting those things which are behind, and reaching forth unto those things which are before, I press toward the mark for the prize of the high calling of God in Christ Jesus" (Philippians 3:13, 14).

You can't talk with him for long before his intense dedication to baseball fades in the face of his even more intense devotion to Jesus Christ and the Christian life.

He doesn't think that his Christianity has given him a better chance to make the team. Because he's a Christian, he says, "I feel that I'm a better person. I don't feel much of a better ballplayer. I can go

97

home and forget about what's happened, not dwell on it, not let it affect my play. That's taking effect from being a Christian. But as far as being a better all-around, tool-wise ballplayer, I don't know that I'm any better. God gave me what He's going to give me, and it's just up to me to refine those tools that He's given me. I don't think that becoming a Christian has given me any other tool."

During spring training, Gruber told reporters that his confidence had increased since the 1985 season. He believed he could do the job – in fact, when he listed his abilities, it would have sounded cocky to anyone who was unaware that he was absolutely accurate – and he believed he deserved a place on the team.

It's unlikely that a year of maturity or experience has been the sole contributing factor to that confidence. One would suspect that an extra year of life as a devout believer had something to do with it as well.

Kelly approaches his faith with the same kind of dedication he brings to almost everything. He is blatantly honest about his own struggles and seems to expect others to be as open about their faith, their successes and their failures.

If a brother on the team seems to be hiding struggles behind a mask of spirituality, Kelly can become quite frustrated, and he's most apt to approach his friend and confront him with the whole matter. There's just the hint of the prophet, and of the pastor, in the man who makes his living playing where they send him.

And they're probably going to send him all over the diamond this year – third base, second base, left field, centre. Kelly won't care as long as they don't send him back to Syracuse!

But even if they did, he'd leave with a gritted-teeth determination to earn his way back. Wise gamblers – which may be a contradiction in terms – wouldn't bet against it.

Chapter 8

Don Gordon

The situation sounded like a set-up for one of those good news/bad news jokes. The good news was that Don Gordon's wife, Deborah, was going to have a baby any day. The bad news was that if Deborah went into labour today or tomorrow, Don would have to miss his first chance in 1986 to pitch for the Toronto Blue Jays.

As he scanned the list of scheduled pitchers for the first game of spring training, posted on the bulletin board in the Blue Jay club house, he saw that he was supposed to come in to pitch relief in the late innings. . . . Unless he wasn't there, of course, because pitching chance or no pitching chance, Deborah and the birth of their first baby were priority one.

He went to bed on the evening of March 7, doubly nervous. The next day would bring either a chance to pitch for the Jays against the Minnesota Twins or a flight to New York to concentrate on another kind of delivery.

Next morning, his spring training roommate, Kelly Gruber, arrived at Grant Field in Dunedin to announce that "Gordie" had caught a 3 a.m. flight north. Not many hours later, Deborah and Don were the proud parents of daughter Christie, and Don didn't have time to worry that he'd missed the Minnesota outing.

Apparently, his excused absense that afternoon had no negative impact on the opinions about Gordon held by Blue Jays management. Don got his chances to pitch and was one of the amazing young crop of hurlers to pitch their way on to an apparently stable pitching staff. He's ecstatic about the opportunity, though he claims it doesn't come close to matching the thrill of his daughter's birth. But he must be especially pleased because his place in the Blue Jays' bullpen is the high point of a fight back from failure.

After a sparkling teenage career played in the heart of New York City, the high school All-American went to the University of South Carolina, where he majored in commercial education and retail management. But he also found time to throw baseballs, and he threw them hard. He led the South Carolina Gamecocks to two consecutive berths in the college World Series in 1981 and 1982.

The pro scouts noticed Gordon, and in June '82 the Detroit Tigers drafted him and assigned him to the Bristol team in the Appalachian league. In 1983 he was promoted to the Birmingham squad, another minor affiliate of Detroit, where he won nine and lost five games that year and registered a career-high 50 strike-outs.

After Detroit's spring training camp in 1984, Don was again sent to Birmingham, where his pitching arm faltered in the early going. By June 23, he had won three and lost two, but his earned run average had soared to 4.97.

But those early struggles didn't prepare Gordon

for the shock that was delivered to him that day – he was informed that he'd been released by Detroit. "Released" is the polite baseball term for "fired" – they didn't need him any longer, and Don was free to do what he liked, as long as that wasn't throwing baseballs for the Tiger organization.

The young man had been married for about nine months at the time; he'd staked his future on success in professional baseball. The next day may have been the longest of his life.

Don remembers it this way: "It was a devastating thing for me. It was a shock. Baseball was something I could always lean on, regardless of whether I was getting along with my family or my girlfriend, regardless of whether I was doing well in school or not, I always had baseball to lean on. That was the one concrete thing in my life."

The concrete had crumbled into dust. But the devastation lasted only for a day or two, thanks, perhaps, to the excellent scouting system of the Toronto Blue Jays. Two days after Detroit cut Gordie he was signed by Toronto as a free agent and assigned to the Syracuse Chiefs.

In his first, partial season, Gordon repeated his won-lost record that had led to his release from Birmingham: three wins and two losses. But the number that impressed everyone was his earned run average. From a high 4.97 earned runs per nine innings in Birmingham, Don reduced his ERA to an excellent 1.79 in Syracuse.

The next season, 1985, the Syracuse pitching staff was close to awesome as Don teamed with the now-legendary "Terminator," Tom Henke, who came to the Blue Jays in late July to help pitch the team to the American League East pennant.

Henke got a lot of positive press – which he deserved – but many of the players who've spent time in Syracuse rank Gordon right there beside him. That in itself is praise for the Jays' organization, because while Gordon is a Detroit cast-off, Henke was released by the Texas Rangers. For that matter, ace starter Doyle Alexander was let go by the Yankees, who have continued to pay the bulk of his salary all the time he was helping the Jays to beat his former teammates, the boys in New York pinstripes.

Jerry Haworth has high praise for Don Gordon, especially in view of the adversity the young pitcher has faced. Haworth says, "I like him. He's someone who's been overshadowed in Syracuse because of Tom Henke's great job. But if Henke hadn't been there, Don Gordon might have been the one to have 25 or 30 saves, and he would have had a lot more publicity.

"He's a sleeper, but he's a great kid, somebody who's faced adversity. He was released by the Tigers, and at that stage a lot of kids go home and that's the end of their careers. But Don said 'No.' "

Despite playing in the shadow of Tom Henke, Don Gordon rang up impressive numbers in Syracuse as a right-handed reliever. He led the club in appearances (51) and was second to Henke in saves (12). He walked the fewest number of opposing batters of any Syracuse pitcher and had the second lowest earned run average on the team, 2.07.

While both media and the fans virtually ignored Gordon in the cloud of glory surrounding Henke, the new star, Jays' management were watching Gordon, and they saw that he was good.

This year he's even better. Along with his friends Mark Eichhorn and Steve Davis (who's been at least temporarily sent back to Syracuse) Don earned an early-season spot in a supposedly set

Blue Jay bullpen. Several positions opened up with injuries to Tom Filer and Gary Lavelle, which put them out for the season but those positions were earned by Gordon and friend Eichhorn with excellent pitching all spring.

And so, less than two years after a major league club told him he was all washed up, Don Gordon at the age of 26 has worked his way onto the roster of another team – the very team that beat out his previous organization for the 1985 American League East championship. It must feel sweet.

And it does. Don Gordon is one happy man. But he tells every reporter who will listen that his happiness doesn't come solely from his successful entrance into the Blue Jays' locker room.

For example, he told John Robertson, the fine writer from The Toronto Sun, that his priorities are: "My God, my family, then baseball." He's said it so often to so many writers and television interviewers – regardless of the ridicule or other fall-out – that it's obvious Gordie means what he's talking about.

The six-foot-one pitcher is an articulate defender of his faith. He explained his involvement with Jesus Christ in these terms:

"Christianity means everything to me. The whole concept of God was a very important thing to me in my whole life.

"I grew up in New York City. My mother was really the biggest influence in my life and in the life of our family, especially in attending church every week. And we said the rosary a lot. We grew up in the Catholic faith and it seemed that I always feared the Lord and always had a relationship with Jesus Christ – but not like I do now."

Like many young people, when Don went to college he left his faith at home.

He describes it: "It just seems that when I got to the later years of high school and in college, there was a kind of void in my Christianity. I still attended church on Sunday, but I was definitely not living with God, in a daily walk with Him. The only time I would call on him to help me was if I was going through a struggle. Then I'd pray. But I didn't have a joyful inner peace like I have now."

It would be hard to dispute that statement. The young man who grew up as a native of the borough of Queens in the most active, frantic city in North America, is laid-back, relaxed and extremely friendly. In a conversation held the day before his wife was due to have their first baby and Don was scheduled to pitch, he was at peace, comfortable and happy. He's obviously telling the truth.

He's also telling the truth – at least, his understanding of it – when he explains that he believes God had something to do with his release by Detroit.

Obviously the Jays thought Detroit had made a mistake in letting him go. They told Don so, and they put their money where their opinions were by signing him.

Gordon says, "Everybody asks me why I was released from Detroit. Everybody in the Blue Jays organization seemed to think I have really good stuff – I think I have good stuff – good enough to be pitching in the major leagues.

"I think my release was a blessing in disguise."

That's the sort of surprising thing Don Gordon frequently says. Instead of expressing anger or frustration at the Tigers, he sees a larger plan unfolding, bigger than any Barfield home run or even a Don Gordon perfect game.

Gordie continues:

"I really think God had something to do with the release, because there wasn't really a good reason for it. I was doing so-so, not really poor or anything like that. I got along great with the organization, with all the managers and all my teammates."

He sees his weaknesses not in terms of pitching skills or team spirit, but in what to him is the most important area of life: his relationship to God. His pattern of turning to God when he was in trouble and turning away when everything was fine again, had continued throughout his minor league career.

"When I'd pitch well, I'd be on top of a mountain. I'd never think of God. I'd attend baseball chapel, but I wasn't living by the Spirit of God. When I was down in my valleys in baseball, I'd call on God to help me out. But then a month later I'd be doing well, and I'd forget about Him again."

"And then, sure enough, June 1984 came around, and I was released."

For Gordon, it was as if his whole world had just collapsed. A professional ballplayer has just one goal: to play in the major leagues. A few aspirants may focus on a particular team, but most would be happy just to get the call-up to any National or American League roster. Everyone recognizes that there's a specific road to that goal: working your way up through the minors.

Don Gordon had just run into a sign that said, "ROAD CLOSED."

He remembered the faith that his mother had known. And he had seen Christianity lived out in the lives of teammates in the Tigers' organization – Christianity that really influenced their lives, not a wishy-washy faith that turned to God only in trouble, as Don had been doing.

Shortly after his release, Don was sitting in a hotel room, holding the broken pieces of a once-promising career in his hands. He had a small New Testament with him, and he picked it up. Before he opened it, he prayed, "Lord, do you want me in this game or not? I'm unhappy. I really feel a burden."

It's a dangerous thing to address God as "Lord"; He might take you seriously. But that's what happened to Don.

He remembers, "In the front of that New Testament was a listing for verses you could turn to in certain situations, like if you were feeling burdened or sad, or when friends fail, and so on. I looked at the first verse listed under 'burdened' – Matthew 11:28."

That verse quotes Jesus, who said, "Come unto Me, all ye who labour and are heavy laden, and I will give you rest."

Those were the very words Don needed to hear. It was as though Jesus had told him that He understood all of Gordon's problems, and He was there to help.

Gordie recalls, "I read that verse and it just jumped out and grabbed me. The moment wasn't a great overcoming; nothing came up and pushed me over or anything like that, but I could just sense the peace and the joy that all these people had been talking about, all the Christians on the team.

"These guys, they just always seemed to be happy. I wanted that so much, you know? And sure enough, when that time came, I just said to Him, 'Jesus, I'm not going to turn my back on You any more. You've helped me in and out, in and out,

107

and now I'm too mature – I understand what the Bible says too much for me to turn away from You now' "

It is significant that when Don talks about that period in his life, he's much more excited about his contract with God than he is about his contract with the Toronto Blue Jays. He figures that when he signed up with the Lord, all the other things God wanted to give him came along as fringe benefits.

He believes he's a better pitcher because he surrendered his life to Jesus.

"Being a Christian really does help me be a better ballplayer. I can't stand it when people say, 'Christians are passive or non-aggressive,' because if anything, as a Christian when you live for the Lord, you want to strive for excellence in whatever you do."

Gordon believes it would dishonour God if he were to do anything less than his best. On those terms, being a Christian guarantees that a player is going to give 100 percent to the club.

Don also thinks it's part of the package for him to try to win and keep his job on the team.

"I believe God has blessed me with the ability to pitch. So many people my age would love to be on the roster of the Toronto Blue Jays. I'm here, and I know it's a blessing, and I'm very thankful for it. I'm going to do whatever I can to hold on to that and to pitch for the Blue Jays."

He admits that the simplistic concept that God will help the believer to beat the non-believer can break down really quickly. It becomes especially tricky if a born-again Christian – say, Don Gordon – is pitching against a born-again Christian – say, one of the Detroit Tigers who shared the good news of Jesus with him in the first place.

Gordon knows that "there's a conflict there. Who is the Lord going to help?" His conclusion, shared by most Christian athletes, is that it's not the specific strike-out or triple that's a gift from God, but the athletic ability. Thus, a Christian who participates in a sport doesn't dishonour God by failing to win; he does bring shame to his Christian witness by failing to try. The Blue Jay rookie pitcher says, the key is "that we play to our abilities."

Two years before Gordon donned a Blue Jays uniform, with number 39 on his back, another Blue Jay reliever named Roy Lee Jackson walked into the dressing room of the Oakland Athletics. It's not normal for a Blue Jay to visit the visitors before the game on game day, but this was a Sunday outing, and Roy Lee had two jobs that afternoon.

In the late innings, Jackson's job was to pitch in relief. But an hour or so before game time, he was the guest speaker at the Oakland chapel service. He pitched well on both occasions. His message to the A's was strong and to the point; he told them they needed Jesus in their lives. He didn't guarantee they would hit home runs; he did guarantee that if they trusted their lives to the Lord, they would find themselves at home, at last.

A couple of hours later, the reliever faced his congregation from the mound. Up to bat came the hard-slugging designated hitter, Dave Kingman. Kingman had lounged in a corner of the chapel while Roy Lee spoke. Jackson gave it his best; so did Kingman. On that day Jackson won – he struck out the impressive long-ball hitter.

Roy Lee would have explained that God didn't want one to strike out and the other to win; the Lord wanted both to do their best.

Roy Lee Jackson and Don Gordon, relievers in the Blue Jays' bullpen, only a couple of years apart, yet in what seem almost to be different eras, would understand each other very well.

Gordie agrees with many of his Blue Jay colleagues about the improvement in mental attitude that can give you a better game, if you are able to entrust your life to God.

He says, "Because I'm a Christian, my mind seems clearer. I have a better understanding of what's going on around me, and I know what I have to accomplish. When I wasn't such a strong Christian, I wasn't really clear about things. I was always trying to figure things out.

"But since I've been letting God take care of things – doing what I can do and letting Him take care of the rest, that too makes me a better ballplayer."

Don is just as concerned to grow as a Christian as he is to improve his pitching. He believes the most important growth factor involves reading the Bible.

He points to other means of growth, as well, but insists they should be secondary: "You can go to hear people speak, you can spend time with your friends, the people whom you have fellowship with, but what you hear is them. But when you read the Bible, that's God talking to you. The Bible is a very personal thing. I don't know if each person takes it exactly the same way, but for me, reading the Bible is the way that I grow the most.

"Sometimes I read, and I don't get anything out of it. I'm just reading words, and I'll put it down. But the times when I'm reading it and I know God is talking to me, that's when I know I'll really grow. I pray that He'll write those words on my heart and keep them there. I pray that the things I don't understand, He'll help me to understand better."

"That communication with God through the Bible is my biggest growth point."

He knows there are other factors in growth as well, and he found the warm and concerned friendships among the born-again Christians on the Toronto Blue Jays squad to be a great bonus for being with the club. This spring was the first time Don encountered some of the Christians, because it was his first time in the Blue Jays' spring training camp, as a member of the club's 40-man roster.

His first impression was, "There are a lot of guys who are Christians, and there are some very strong Christians."

He finds that this makes sincere and meaningful communication very possible – he could talk about living as a Christian and about the Bible, and he found "it's not like you're talking to the dark. Somebody will understand what you're saying, and possibly even clear you up on it if you're saying something wrong. In that respect, it really helps."

According to Gordon, baseball is a great environment in which to grow as a Christian. That may seem strange to some, because the sport also presents a multitude of temptations to its practitioners. But the new pitcher says, "In a baseball atmosphere, you're around the guys in pretty much a relaxed atmosphere for a large part of the day. Whereas somebody who works an average job – and believe me, I've worked at plenty of jobs – doesn't have the opportunity to simply reach out and grab somebody and say, 'Hey Ron, clear me up on this,' or 'Jesse, what do you think about this?' or 'Kelly, what are your thoughts on this?'

"I think this kind of atmosphere is really great. I really feel blessed. I couldn't wait to have fellow-

111

ship with the guys."

It's tough to ignore Don Gordon. He's so sure of his faith and so committed to sharing it that the fact that he's a Christian is going to influence everything he does. He's concerned that he will be able to "witness effectively," to share what he's found with the people around him.

That doesn't always make for relaxed relationships, especially with people who are cautious about "born-again" Christians. After he made his life-changing decision, Don's first challenge was his wife, Deborah.

He remembers: "My wife was slow to turn to the Lord. She was like me – she went to church when she was younger, but didn't have the day-to-day fellowship with the Lord."

But the Gordon marriage is based in deep affection and warm friendship – you don't have to be with Don long before you realize that's true. His wife Deborah was was also his friend, and she noticed some significant changes in her new husband – they'd been married only a few months when Don made his commitment to serve Christ. Not all of the changes made her completely comfortable.

But, not long ago, she decided that she wanted what her husband had found, and Don says, "Now she really understands, and she's saying a lot of prayers, and the Holy Spirit has really come on strong with her.

"We're on the same wave length, whereas a year ago I was AM and she was FM."

Gordon says that being at spiritual unity has helped an already successful marriage: "Even though we got along great before, this has just improved it that much more."

112

The Gordons are committed as well to raising Christie to love God. Don eagerly awaits the time when he and Deborah can begin to teach their young child about God and to lead her to faith in Christ.

His marriage isn't the only relationship affected by his faith. Don is aware that the Christians in the Blue Jays club house are seen as being different, but he's sensed no real negative reaction.

Asked if there's prejudice against the believers on the squad, he says, "I've never experienced that so far. But it has crossed my mind; I've wondered.

"Just the other day Kelly and Jeff and I were asking each other, 'I wonder how they perceive us. Do they look at us as passive, or what?' "

This concern with being considered passive surfaces constantly in conversations with athletes who are also born-again Christians. The evidence indicates that it isn't true, that each of them is determined to give 100 percent on the playing field, and yet they're aware of the rumoured rap that's against them.

But it's unlikely that the three men who were involved in the conversation will ever accurately be accused of non-aggressiveness. Gruber, Gordon and Hearron are intense, take-charge guys, ready to play day in and day out.

Gordon believes that some misunderstood – or simply mistaken – teachings have contributed to the myth of the wimpy Christian sports figure. He says, "I think in some instances there are guys who say, 'Well, I struck out, and that's God's will.'

"Well, I think that's wrong, and I think they need to be straightened out on that. I think someone who acts that way might jeopardize everybody else who's a Christian."

113

But if the Christians continue to contribute at full throttle, Don thinks that will be just fine with the Blue Jays front office. He says, "I really don't think it would turn the management off. For one thing, you're going to get somebody who's giving 100 percent. You're going to have somebody who's honest, who'll give a hard day's work every day. You can count on people like that."

He believes that this is the ethic taught in the Bible: "Colossians 3:23 says, 'Work as though you're working for the Lord.' We're to serve our earthly masters as we'd serve God."

But there's always the "what if" – what if his strong faith offended people enough that he was dropped or traded, something that's happened to other athletes in a number of sports.

Gordie smiles with confidence. He declares, "God has a greater plan than any man. I believe that if my testimony did jeopardize my job, I should just think of Jesus, who, even before He was crucified, was spat on and everything else, by all the people. If He can go through that, a baseball player can go through a few derogatory remarks about being a Christian. No problem."

It seems unlikely that his faith will be an issue on the Jays. First he's one of a hefty handful of born-again Christians who are making a significant impact on the baseball field. One game early in the season saw six of the men featured in this book take to the field to start the game.

Second, Gordon's pitching has been good enough that nobody is looking for reasons to criticize him. He's impressed everyone in spring training, and his ERA has remained low. Blue Jays management have stated that Gordon has nothing more to prove – he had earned his way onto the team by the mid-point of the exhibition games in the spring, and he'll stay in the big league uniform as long as he keeps doing the job and stays "hungry," in the words of manager Jimy Williams.

May saw a probably temporary return to Syracuse for Don. But his assortment of pitches – his fastball, a sinker, a slider and a forkball among them – have worked well. And as long as he does the job on the mound, the management probably won't care if he preaches from the right field bleachers on his days off.

Chapter 9

Jeff Hearron

Jeff Hearron is doing it the hard way.

Almost everyone in the know – except maybe Jeff himself – believes that Hearron is a season or two away from really being ready for the major leagues. Possibly no position on the baseball diamond requires more seasoning than Hearron's – crouching behind home plate as one of the Blue Jays' catchers. Catchers not only have to worry about their own hitting and fielding – the major concerns of the other non-pitchers – but also about pitching. It's the catcher who calls the game, choosing the pitches and working closely with the pitchers. It's demanding mental and physical work.

The "battery" – pitcher and catcher – is a challenging enough job that pitchers and catchers report to spring training camp a week before the rest of the players. Catchers often come up to the big leagues a couple of years later than other members of the team; they need the time to hone the multiple skills needed to play their important role in the game.

Jeff should have had those extra years as well. That was part of the Blue Jays' game plan for their young catcher. But he lost some of those extra games to injury and has come to the big club sooner than planned because of the physical problems of Blue Jays veteran catchers Ernie Whitt and Buck Martinez.

In mid-July 1985 Buck Martinez was the loser in a spectacular home plate collision with Seattle's Phil Bradley. When they got Buck into X-ray, they found his right ankle dislocated and his leg broken.

Martinez earned the undying respect of baseball fans everywhere with his heroic reaction to the crash. Although in terrible pain, he held on to the ball to tag Bradley out, attempted a wild throw to third base and then, on a return toss from third, tagged out yet another runner trying to come home against the now-prone catcher. If there's a place in the record books for a successful double-play by a catcher with his leg broken in two or more places, Martinez would be the only entry.

That catastrophe left the Jays with only one catcher, Ernie Whitt. Whitt played well for the rest of the season, but catching is exhausting work, and most baseball observers believe the challenge took its toll on the 33-year-old Whitt. In August Jeff Hearron was called up as Whitt's back-up. Although Jeff appeared in only four games of the regular season, the 24-year-old also saw limited action in two games of the play-offs, thus earning the envy of other junior Jays who'd been sent home by the time the Kansas City series began.

Almost no one believed that Martinez, now 37, could work his way back into top physical condition and thus return to the demanding catcher's role for the Blue Jays. But he did so and started this season with the Jays in fine form – stage two of the heroic story of Buck Martinez.

His return allowed the club to send Jeff back to the minor leagues, where he'd played AA ball in Knoxville in 1984 and most of 1985. His first professional season, 1983, was at Florence in the South Atlantic League.

But Jeff's return to the minors didn't last long. Martinez was apparently healthy, but colleague Ernie Whitt experienced back spasms and wound up on the disabled list. California native Jeff Hearron once again headed for the bracing climate of Toronto in April of this year and began the season playing a regular shift behind home plate. Jeff didn't burn up the league in hitting, but he was respectable, celebrating his first major league double against the Baltimore Orioles on April 26. He converted the double into a run scored in that important game.

If there's a weakness with the Jays this year, it certainly appears to be at the catcher's position. Both Whitt and Martinez are still physically suspect and Hearron is inexperienced. But Jeff's determined to do his job and to prove that he deserves to be in the majors, even at the young age (for a catcher) of 24. Some believe he's indeed begun to prove himself and therefore deserves a spot on the squad even if both veteran catchers were healthy.

Knowledgeable baseball observers believe Hearron will eventually find a permanent place in the major leagues, perhaps as number 54 for the Toronto Blue Jays.

Broadcaster Jerry Haworth, who's certainly a keen baseball observer, says, "If it weren't for the injuries, he'd probably be a little more advanced in his career, but he's young and he's patient. He handles himself well and he's good with the pitchers. You need that kind of chemistry when you're working with a pitching staff.

"He has good ability, so everything's in place. It might take him another couple of years, but I think he's got the patience and the knowledge to someday be a major league catcher."

But for sections of the '86 season, it's high-pressure on-the-job training for Jeff Hearron.

His professional career has actually been very short. In 1983 he was still in university, playing for the University of Texas at Austin. His team won the national championship that year, and Hearron demonstrated the kind of talent for the game that attracted the attention of the Blue Jays' scouts. That year he batted .341, hit six home runs and was named catcher on the All-Western Conference team.

But his body threw a curve at him in '84. Jeff suffered a torn right rotator cup injury and went on a long rehabilitation program – he could certainly sympathize with Buck Martinez. When he got the call from the Jays in August of '85, he was still working his way back to full strength in the injured shoulder.

Hearron came into spring training '86 in good health, with his shoulders – and the rest of him – in great shape. His hobby, swimming, certainly contributed to his return to full health. In fact, almost all of the Jays showed up for the first day of training camp in close to mid-season condition. These guys take their business seriously. During spring training, manager Jimy Williams compliments his players: "The frame of mind of a lot of these players is excellent."

Like his friends Mark Eichhorn and Kelly Gruber, Jeff Hearron is a bachelor. While that undoubtedly eases the pressure of the kind of commuter career that the young catcher has had so far, it also makes for a more lonely life-style. But the catcher, pitcher and third baseman spend a lot of time together at training camp and in Toronto.

Hearron knows that at this point in his career it's the circumstances and not just his skills that have put him in a Blue Jays' uniform. He understands the training process for catchers and didn't expect to advance beyond AA ball in 1985. The Syracuse AAA team wasn't in his plans, let alone Toronto and a locker in Exhibition Stadium.

That's not to say that he wasn't overjoyed at the prospect.

Jeff remembers the night he got the word from the big club: "The highlight of my career so far has to be last year, when I was called up. It was really ironic, because last year was a rehabilitation year for me – I was coming off shoulder surgery. Just before I got called up I was playing every day. I had been for about two weeks, but before that I was playing only once every four days.

"I remember my roommate was out. It was fairly late, about 11 o'clock, and I got down on my knees and asked the Lord some questions like, 'Why am I in this game? Show me; you know I want to be in your will.' "

It won't come as a surprise to the readers of this book that Jeff Hearron, too, is a Christan. He became a born-again believer after being the victim in an accident. More about that to follow – but back to Jeff's story of his call-up to the Blue Jays.

"I really got into some prayer heavily for about an hour. Then I was awakened the next morning by a phone call."

The call was from Blue Jays' third base coach John McLaren, who said directly: "Pack your bags.

You're going to the big leagues.

Jeff remembers that it didn't quite register at first. "I was half asleep and I just said, 'What?' "

The coach repeated the news: "Pack your bags. You're going to the big leagues."

Jeff was in shock. "I couldn't believe this. I hung up the phone and took a shower, and I was saying, 'Lord, You're awesome, You're great.' At the time I was so happy and content being in Double A – not that I didn't want to be in Triple A or Toronto, but I was content with where the Lord had me at that time. I was just trying to serve Him at the AA level. That was the highlight of my year last year, both spiritually and in terms of baseball."

Hearron has known the Christian life since he was a child, but he admits that he really became serious about his faith after a traumatic incident involving a potentially serious automobile accident.

He says, "I accepted the Lord when I was in sixth grade, but I guess I really didn't live a Christian life until maybe a year and a half ago when I got into an accident while riding a bicycle. I was hit by a drunk driver, and that day I lay on the ground bleeding, not seriously hurt, but knowing that my life could have been taken. The Lord spared my life.

"That's when I knew I had to dedicate my life to the Lord and just have fun knowing Him."

That final phrase may seem to be a marked departure from the tone that the conversation had taken until then. But Jeff insists that being a Christian is anything but boring. He's truly having fun serving the Lord.

The young catcher says, "I guess a lot of non-Christians might think it's a drag living the Christian life. And I guess if you're not a Christian, it could be a drag having to go to church and be holy or whatever.

"But being a Christian doesn't mean you can't have fun or joke around. I'm just having fun in the Lord. It's a great life."

It's a great life to Jeff Hearron because there's a lot of joy, but also because of the security he knows in his faith. He defines Christianity simply:

"Christianity means knowing Jesus Christ as my Saviour, that my sins are forgiven and that I'll see Him face to face some day."

Obviously, Hearron likes to have fun. As a young rookie he's also the victim of jokes from the veteran players. He takes all of that in stride.

One example of the slightly mocking humour of the dugout is his nickname – "Hank." That comes from the resemblance between his name – Hearron – and that of the great slugger, Hank Aaron (H. Aaron). But it's also a friendly insult to the man who, until the '86 season began, had played only five major league games. Jeff takes it very lightly.

But he doesn't take his job lightly. One of the toughest assignments that befalls a catcher is blocking home plate, to prevent a runner from trying to score from third base. That can lead to a lot of full-tilt collisions, such as the two-truck pile-up that sidelined Buck Martinez in 1985.

In short, a catcher has to be aggressive and willing to take a considerable pounding. In fact, a catcher must be downright brave, because in addition to cutting runners off at the pass, he must also be willing to face foul tips, wild pitches, and free-swinging tips of swung bats. At times, crouching ahead of the umpire is about as attractive as fighting bulls barehanded.

Hearron has both the aggressiveness and the courage for the job. In fact, his description of his style of play might almost leave him open to the opposite criticism.

"Being a Christian doesn't mean I can't take a guy out at second. Or if I strike out, it doesn't mean I have to come back and lay my helmet down easy, put my bat in the rack and say, 'Well, it was God's will.'" He's bluntly honest: "I think that's baloney. I don't believe that. I think I'm a competitor, I'm a battler and I'll fight and scratch and kick to win a ball game. Winning a ball game isn't everything, but I would like to be successful, and I strive for perfection. I think Jesus would do the same. He got angry a few times, but didn't sin. I think we can be angry and not sin. The Bible tells us we can do that."

That leaves little question regarding Hearron's aggressiveness. Concerning the need for courage, Jeff believes faith helps him to deal with fear.

"I think a Christian ballplayer has a little advantage about not really having many fears. A hitter can't really stand at the plate and have a fear of the ball. You can't be afraid that it'll hit you, or you're not going to be successful.

"The Lord can take that fear away, if you ask Him."

Like many of his teammates, Jeff is quick to admit that he hasn't found perfection either as a ballplayer or as a Christian. He has one weakness that he doesn't like to talk about, but one of his teammates tells this story on the solidly built catcher.

Apparently Jeff is the product of the minor league – and especially southern United States – baseball culture. And in his younger days, part of the equipment, right along with glove and mask, was chewing tobacco. There is still a good supply, in a variety of brands, in the club house refrigerator.

Jeff admitted to his Christian brothers that he should give up that habit, but he's been unable to do so. His most extreme attempt saw him absolutely pack his mouth with the stuff, chew and chew and chew and then – hold your stomach – swallow the lot.

He was sufficiently forward-thinking to conduct the experiment over a large garbage can in the team's dressing room. But while he may have felt a bit queasy, it didn't work. He wasn't sick, and he has yet to abandon the habit.

It may seem strange to include such a story in a book about role models such as these members of the Jays, but one of the most compelling things about these men, each and every one, is their honesty about their own failings. None of them claims to be an ideal person – but each one is an honest man, dealing with his own personal failings and weaknesses with God's help.

Each of them would understand the popular motto: "Please be patient; God's not through with me yet." None of them would say, "Look at me"; instead they would insist that you "Look at Jesus Christ."

At the time of writing, Jeff had already accomplished his goal for the season, although he did so through the back door of injury to the Blue Jays' catchers. His first aim was to make the squad.

Yet he regrets the circumstances that opened a temporary spot on the team – he has genuine affection and a lot of respect for both Ernie Whitt and Buck Martinez. When both became healthy, Jeff was sent back to the minors. At this point in his career – and in his spiritual growth – that's OK with him.

He says, "My goal is to make the team. But if not, I'll go one step lower, to Syracuse. If not there, if the Lord wants me in Knoxville again, I'll go to Knoxville for a third year."

But his aggressiveness re-emerges, even when he talks about his career. "I'd like to set my goals high and say, 'Toronto.' " For at least part of this season, he's hit his goal.

Chapter 10

Steve Davis

Steve Davis is deeply disappointed. He started the season as one of the ten pitchers on the Toronto Blue Jays' roster, filling one of the spaces – along with Mark Eichhorn and Don Gordon – opened up by the injury problems to Gary Lavelle, Tom Filer and Bill Caudill.

But each of the new Jays was aware that, while Lavelle and Filer were out for the season, Caudill would be back, and others such as Stan Clarke and Luis Leal in the minor system might also threaten their job security.

Near the end of April the crunch came; Caudill returned to active duty, and Davis lost the lottery. He was sent down to Syracuse to further refine his pitching skills, the one road trip he had been hoping to avoid in 1986.

But though immediate disappointment is inevitable, Steve probably has very little to worry about in the long run. The young pitcher who will turn 26 on August 4 has had a dream career so far.

Baseball America magazine picked Davis as one of the 16 top major league rookie prospects for 1986. He was one of nine young pitchers to make that list.

The article called him "a quality lefthanded starter . . . the only twenty-game winner in the minor leagues last year." He was also the first 20-game winner in the Blue Jays organization, finishing the season with a composite record of 22 wins and nine losses, divided among the three clubs he served in his race for the top.

Steve entered his fifth professional baseball season this spring, but he feels as though he's hurtled through the minors right to the major league level. That's especially true because in 1985 he pitched 27 games at Knoxville (Double A), moved to Triple A at syracuse for only 6 games, and then was called up to the parent club in Toronto, where he pitched well in clutch situations during the Blue Jays' penant drive.

He chalked up a two wins-one loss record for the Jays, starting five games and appearing in five more.

He was thrilled when he got the call from the Blue Jays in August of 1984. But when the Jays originally drafted Davis in 1982, he wasn't sure how he should react.

He remembers, "Well, they weren't doing too well at the time. I really had no idea of what to expect, although just being drafted was certainly a highlight."

But as Steve moved up through the minors season by season, the Jays were moving up even faster in the divisional standings. Davis began his professional career as a relief pitcher in Medicine Hat, Alberta, the Blue Jays' farm club in the Pioneer League. But the next year, he became a starting pitcher on the Florence squad, the role in which he feels most comfortable. He sees himself as a starter.

He remembers that 1983 season, in which he played a starting role: "I had a really good season, and I was moved up to Double A right at the end of the season. That was a big highlight."

The Blue Jays are also hoping that Davis will eventually earn his way into the starting line-up. The Jays have traditionally been short-staffed in their supply of left-handed pitchers. Left-hander Jimmy Key was the first in several seasons to have much success, and the Jays are hoping Davis will complement Key.

If Davis returns to the Jays this season, it will once again be as a relief pitcher. But manager Jimmy Williams believes he could eventually be a starting hurler. Williams says that although his initial period of service will be in the bullpen, "that's not to say that in time he may not be a starter. Personally, I like him as a starter and I think his niche in the game will be as a starter. But if you reflect back on Jimmy Key, you'll know that originally, when he first came up here, he was used in the bullpen. Of course, we put him in as a starter last year, and it's worked out very well for him."

Comparisons with the talented Key seem to be inevitable, and Key's path to success may possibly be the same road followed by Davis.

Steve doesn't mind bullpen work, but he certainly is giving everything he has to ensure that his bullpen work will once again be for the major league club.

As one sportswriter asked last season, "How will you keep Steve Davis down on the farm team in Syracuse, once he's seen Toronto?"

Steve reflects on his phenomenal '85 season: "I started out in Double A again, and things went beyond what I expected. I won so many games that I had 17 wins before I left there at the end of July, and one thing led to another.

"I moved up to Triple A. I think I deserved it because I had done well enough, but the biggest highlight was getting called up to the big leagues. The day I found out was a very happy day for me, because I thought to myself, 'I've been working so hard for so many years to achieve this goal, and here it is today.' "

How many years? Steve says he began working toward pitching major league baseball when he was six years old!

He says that when his chance came to pitch in the big leagues, he didn't go on an ego trip: "I didn't pat myself on the back and say, 'I'm so great.' It was just a great feeling inside, a happy moment. I couldn't believe it. I was on the plane going to Toronto, and I had to pinch myself: 'Man, I'm going to the big leagues, I can't believe this.' "·

And what did he find when he checked into the Blue Jays' clubhouse, where his uniform, number 25, hung on a locker? "Once I got up there, I found out that everybody was just like everyone else, normal people – except that they're great baseball players."

Odds are good that, despite his mid-season setback this year, Steve Davis will also be known as a great ballplayer before too long.

His first game in the majors is good evidence of his potential. Playing against Chicago, he took his first batter out on a pop-up to the catcher. In fact, he sent down the first twelve batters he faced! That start gave him a great infusion of confidence, a commodity Steve didn't lack in the first place.

Jerry Haworth notes Davis' potential: "Steve is very confident; he exudes a lot of enthusiasm. He's somebody who's learned the art of pitching, and even though he has a lot more to learn, he could be a tremendous starter in the Blue Jays' rotation. They say he may surpass Jimmy Key, who may be one of the finest young lefthanders in all of major league baseball.

"Steve's learned to be a little more aggressive, he works the plate very well, he's got good tools, and he's a good pupil. He listens well. I can see in him a man who's got a lot of self-confidence. He's unpretentious, and at his age, with all of the success he's had, he's also had some times when he wasn't too successful. He's had to earn his spurs." He's been given an opportunity to sharpen those spurs just a little more this season.

Haworth also points to a less obvious attribute: "He has a great wife, and you need a great wife in this profession." Steve married Kelly on February 25, 1984. She's a petite, pretty woman who's moved with Steve to whatever club he was assigned to – and there have been numerous stops in the last couple of years, most of them on the "up" elevator.

Steve's success may have come as a surprise even to the dedicated pitcher himself. He was chosen well down in the Free Agent Draft in 1982 – the Jays picked him up as the 523rd choice overall (their 21st selection), which is hardly an auspicious beginning for a major league pitching career.

Haworth says that you can tell a lot about Davis's determination by his reaction to being chosen so low in the draft: "He was chosen at the bottom, but here he is at the major league level. That tells you a little bit about his intestinal fortitude."

Davis is a bright, cheerful, youthful-looking ballplayer. Although he's six foot one and weighs 183, his blonde hair and ample supply of freckles leave the impression of an irrepressible kid. Obviously his teammates agree with that assessment – his nickname is "Jody" – he's named for the small boy on the now-defunct television program, "Family Affair."

Steve's optimistic outlook and dedication to the game arise at least partly from his Christian faith. He's not the most outspoken of the believers on the Jays, but there's no question about his commitment to his faith.

He says, "I'm not the kind of guy who's going to get up in front of 50 people and say, 'I'm a Christian.' But if a discussion gets close to that topic, and if I'm talking to one guy, I'll start talking about it. I'm not afraid to tell somebody that I'm a Christian, and I'm very happy about it. I'm not the best one, but I care enough to try."

And while he'd never seek an opportunity to speak to a few dozen people, Steve eagerly cooperated in the preparation of this book.

Davis first encountered Christianity in his second year of college, at Texas A&M University, near his hometown of San Antonio, where he and Kelly still live in the off-season. While at college, Steve met a committed Chirstian who, says the left-handed pitcher, "just opened my eyes to Christianity. He made me think for the first time that there really is something to it."

He didn't make any quick decision and confesses that "I didn't know if I was ready to commit to it." But the words of his friends stuck with him, and when he hit a low point in his life during the next fall, he realized that he'd been offered his answer:

"Things weren't going well; I was mad at myself. I wasn't manic-depressive, but I was really down. I sat down and asked Jesus to become my Saviour, because I found out I needed help. I found I can't control my destiny day after day. Somebody else has that power."

He's maintained that commitment, although Steve admits that he sometimes fails to uphold his side of the relationship. He confesses that, on a busy day, it's easy to place Bible reading or prayer low on the priority list.

His greatest encouragement, he finds, comes from other believers on the ball club: "Having a lot of people feeling the same way helps, because it's good to talk with other people. If I were the only one here, I'd still be a Christian, but I don't know if I'd be as strong, because I wouldn't have fellowship, interaction with other people."

Steve places a lot of importance on the weekly baseball chapel services, especially because the players find it impossible to maintain regular church attendance during the season. He says, "I enjoy baseball chapel quite a bit, because it gives us a chance to get together. It's a good, short message, and it's enjoyable."

Chaplain David Fisher says that the 1985 chapel included a solid core of believers who met each week. About nine players would turn up for chapel each week – often held in the weight room next to the Blue Jays' locker room. He terms that group "a good solid nucleus. It was the most solid nine that we've ever had."

The chapel program is open to all of the players, coaches and managers. The only "outsiders" who attend are the chaplain and the day's guest speaker, frequently a former professional athlete like hockey player Paul Henderson or Canadian Football League star Gord Barwell, both of whom are now involved in Christian ministries on a full-time basis. While the players' wives don't attend the chapel, they do spend a lot of time together. Marla Barfield and Kelly Davis have become close.

Fisher believes that the friendship that arises from chapel attendance can change attitudes of the players, who are often in competition with one another as well as with the opposing teams.

He points to an example involving Davis: "Last summer Steve Davis had a place opened up on the roster because of Gary Lavelle's elbow problems. But I remember that Steve wasn't hoping that Gary's elbow would stay bad. Steve was pulling for Gary."

Steve agrees with that assessment, but admits that players' situations can be emotionally complicated. Lavelle is out again this year for the season with continuing arm problems. At training camp it was possible that Davis would take his place. Steve commented on the situation:

"I'm sorry that his arm is bothering him. He's a friend of mine, and I'm sorry things aren't working out for him, and I hope they will. But if I were to replace him, I would have to go at it full force. Not that I'm trying to do better than him because he's hurt, but it's an opportunity that I'd like to have."

He believes that Lavelle would support that position: "I'm sure he does. I know him well enough – he's the type of person who's supportive of everybody. He really cares about other people and how they do."

Steve argues that while God hasn't made him a better pitcher since he became a believer, he still owes his career to the Lord. "I think He had something in mind for me a long time ago. From the first time I started playing baseball, I really felt that something was on my side. I never knew what it was, but everything always worked out for me.

"Granted, I've had bad games, and I've had a not-so-good season, but for some reason I've kept coming back and doing well. God has helped me out quite a bit."

He says he was always aware that God was giving him the good things that happened to him. "Even before I became a Christian, I knew that everything was out of my hands, and I always thought that the best thing was going to work out for me. Things are going to happen for me the way they're supposed to, and I really can't control them too much."

Steve knows he has to do his job and work his hardest. If the experts are right, that should be enough to get him back to the majors in short order. His goal, of course, is to play with the Blue Jays again, and once again Steve Davis has a goal he's likely to attain.

Chapter 11

Gary Lavelle

When the season records for 1986 are published, Gary Lavelle's numbers will probably consist of an asterisk and not much more. The veteran relief pitcher has been sidelined for the entire season by a recurring elbow problem. The same ailment that cost him parts of the 1983 and 1985 seasons also forced him into surgery in the early days of the '86 campaign.

The man affectionately known as "Pudge" (which is hardly fair, since he's six foot one and 200 pounds) came to training camp in the spring of '86 feeling ready to pitch and hoping that the preceding season's problems that plagued him were over, but he again blew out his left arm throwing batting practice in Florida.

The recurrence of his injury was a blow to the Blue Jays. Manager Jimy Williams said, "We definitely need a quality lefthanded pitcher such as Lavelle in our bullpen. He's had the experience, and we counted on him very much for 1986."

But the Jays have had to go to Plan B, because Lavelle is gone for the year. When his pitching arm failed to improve, Gary was scheduled for minor, arthroscopic exploratory surgery in Los Angeles.

But the doctors discovered extensive ligament damage and actually removed a tendon from Lavelle's calf and used it to replace torn ligaments in the elbow.

The operation has been used successfully to treat other pitchers, including Tommy John, who've returned to successful careers. But for Lavelle, who turned 37 on January 3, to continue in his chosen profession as a relief pitcher is at best a major challenge, and at worst a dead-end street. Such an effort will take a great deal of determination and a few positive breaks.

Jerry Haworth recognizes that this might be the blow that ends Lavelle's 13-year major league career after a total of 716 big league appearances. He says, "I feel sorry for Gary this year. With his left elbow, and at his age, his career might be over."

Even if that's so, Gary Lavelle can be proud of his contribution to baseball. He's a relative newcomer to the Toronto Blue Jays, traded to the club from the San Francisco Giants before the 1985 season in return for Blue Jays pitchers Jim Gott and Jack McKnight, and infielder Augie Schmidt. He was expected to be a hero in the bullpen, but he struggled at times during the season, winding up with five wins and seven losses, and an earned run average of 3.10. He survived an especially miserable period in mid-July, pitching in relief for three consecutive games and being posted as the losing pitcher of record each time, twice to California and once to the Oakland A's.

Observers suggest that Gary had some difficulty in adapting to his new club. His entire career had been spent with the San Francisco Giants, beginning in the minor leagues in 1967 (with Salt Lake City), moving up through the league levels with stops at such baseball hotbeds as Medford, Decatur, Amarillo and Phoenix, and hurling for the Giants every season from 1987 through 1984.

He set relief records with San Francisco, including most saves (127) and most appearances (647), which surpassed the mark set by great Christy Matthewson.

His entry in the Blue Jays media guide covers more than a page, the length itself attesting to his endurance and his talent. Blue Jays fans have yet to see Lavelle consistently at his best – and now, with his powerful left arm in a sling in his twentieth season as a professional ballplayer, this one played entirely in "idle" gear – they may never see Gary pitch at his finest. That would especially be a shame because Jays' fans, normally among the most courteous in the league, had few cheers for the struggling reliever during 1985.

But despite all of his struggles last season, Gary Lavelle has proved himself to be one of the finest reliefers in baseball over the past decade and a half. One of his greatest moments occurred in 1977, when Lavelle pitched two innings in the All-Star game, yielding no runs and only one hit, and striking out major long-ball threats Reggie Jackson and Carl Yastrzemski. He was also selected to the 1983 National League All-Star squad but was unable to play.

Gary opened the 1976 season in fine style, going 18 innings without yielding a run and 35 innings with only one runner crossing home plate. He played a part in the first seven Giants' wins that season, pitching as the "stopper" – the relief pitcher who comes in to nail down the victory in the late innings of a close game, the role handled so well in late 1985 by Blue Jay Tom Henke.

In 1978 Lavelle led the National League in relief victories, with 13. His role has been exclusively that of reliever – he didn't start a game in the major leagues until 1981, when his first starting assignment followed 434 relief efforts.

He's played an important role in a lot of great ball games. But Gary Lavelle may never step onto a mound and squint over his prominent nose to pick up the sign from the catcher again. Some ballplayers turn to Christianity when they face a crisis like this. Gary doesn't have to – because his Christian faith is as much a part of him as his pitching arm. And as he would tell you, God doesn't fail him even if his left elbow does.

Haworth finds Lavelle's outspoken faith in Christ to be one of the key elements that make up the man. The broadcaster speaks from personal friendship with Lavelle: "Gary said, 'If God wants me to pitch, I'll pitch.' He's someone who says, 'God has directed my life.' He's a great family man, with great kids.

"I've learned a lot about the Bible through Gary. He's probably the most well-spoken ambassador for Christ I've ever met on a baseball field; he shares his information and he's fun to listen to. I love Gary Lavelle, and if his arm doesn't come around, I know he'll be a great contributor in his community and his job."

Haworth speaks with affection and warmth – he's obviously seen character and personality in Lavelle that he likes a lot. He's not alone in that – Gary seems to have that effect on people. The younger members of the Jays have nothing but good things to say about the veteran pitcher. And chapel coordinator David Fisher says, "Gary's one of the first guys I ever knew in baseball. Back in the late '70s he was with the Giants, and they had a bunch of guys they called the God Squad. Gary was chapel leader with the Giants for a long time.

"I started going to Montreal in 1976, and I met him there. There was a closeness that developed between us then, and I could sense a real maturity in him. He was someone I really felt comfortable with. We wouldn't talk about all the peripheral things; we'd talk about the meaty things of the Christian life – discipleship, getting involved in a local church, really serious stuff. I've always sensed a lot of wisdom when I've talked with Gary.

"I think he helped me more than I helped him. There were times when I'd go to Montreal more than anything else just to have breakfast or supper with Gary Lavelle. He's one of my closest friends in baseball."

Gary may not be able to make pitches this season, but there's no doubt that he'll continue to make friends. Nonetheless, the change from his team of almost two decades to the young Toronto Blue Jays was a difficult transition for the popular ex-Giant.

Fisher offers this opinion: "I think coming to the Blue Jays was traumatic for him, because he spent all his career in a different league, and all with one team. It took him most of the season before he really found himself fitting in, even with the Christians on the team."

Those adjustments eventually sorted themselves out, and Gary optimistically looked forward to a better '86. Fisher remembers when he realized that Gary had settled in as a Blue Jay: "By the end of the season he'd grown close to the guys. In the final chapel, he said that the Christians on the Blue Jays were the closest group of Christians he'd ever en-

139

countered in baseball."

And what does Gary Lavelle have to say about Gary Lavelle? He sits nursing his arm and explains that although he loves playing the game of baseball, his pitching ability isn't the key to happiness.

"Basically, I have to go back to what my foundation is. My foundation is Jesus Christ my Lord, and I believe that God's going to have me where He best wants me, and if it's to be in baseball, I'll get better and I'll be able to pitch, and if not, I'm sure He'll tell me where He wants me to be."

That's not hype for the consumption of a media type – Gary really believes what he says, and he's followed that path of faith since his second season with the Giants.

Like many of his Blue Jay teammates, he found the Lord through friendship with another ballplayer. It's just that the encounter took place for Gary while his new friends in Toronto were largely still in grade school!

Gary recalls the decision which he says altered every facet of his existence: "Back in November 1975 I accepted the Lord in Venezuela. It happened through a friend of mine who witnessed to me, Tom Johnson, who pitched for the Minnesota Twins. We were there playing winter baseball and became friends, and he started sharing with me about a relationship he had with Jesus Christ.

"I started asking him a lot of questions about life in general, and I just decided one day that if Jesus Christ was who He said He was, then I wanted to know Him as my Lord and Saviour. I invited Him into my heart at that time."

His decision made little difference in Lavelle's abilities as a ballplayer. His stats sheet shows that he had an earned run average of 2.12 in 1974, before his sojourn in South America, 2.96 in '75, and 2.70 in '76. But Gary wasn't making deals with God to improve his pitching – it was already just fine. This was something bigger, involving his entire existence.

When he talks about the impact of his new relationship with Jesus Christ, he doesn't even mention baseball: "It totally changed my life. It gave me a new direction and really gave me the understanding of why we're here. My whole attitude toward life changed, and I started realizing that we were meant to have fellowship with God. Our reason for being here is to glorify God in all that we do and say, and to have fellowship with Him."

This was a really radical change of direction for someone who'd already experienced the life of a professional baseball player for eight seasons. But you have only to talk to Gary for a few moments to realize that those changes have stuck with him. His relationship with Christ now dominates his life, and he also thinks that the changes had a definite impact on his chosen profession.

"I think my attitude started changing in the way I approach things. My attitude to baseball changed, because I believe that God endowed me with the ability. Now I was to use it for His glory and praise rather than for my own glory."

During a long and successful career, there have certainly been opportunities of glory for Gary. But he's determined to redirect any praise to his heavenly Father.

He didn't do that by winning ball games. He did it by being a genuine, honest, humble man and a dedicated follower of his Lord. It's unlikely that anyone has given glory to God when Gary Lavelle has saved a game, but the comments by men such as Jerry Haworth and David Fisher show how much impact his off-field life and his quiet, yet eager testimony of personal faith has had on people he's met.

Christians are often accused of being judgmental and critical. Lavelle believes he's gone in the opposite direction. "I think I started understanding people better, why people do some of the things they do and get involved in some of the things they shouldn't be involved in. I think my whole understanding of life changed, definitely for the better."

His priorities also changed. As Haworth said, Lavelle is a dedicated family man. He and his wife Regina have been married for 14 years, and they have two children – Jana and Timothy. He's also dedicated to Christian ministries to athletes, and his Blue Jay biography notes that he's an active member of the Fellowship of Christian Athletes. (Gary's bio is the only one of the Jays to note his Christian activities).

In addition, it's quickly apparent that Gary is a loyal and involved American citizen – perhaps another reason why moving to the Blue Jays caused culture shock. He served for six years in the National Guard and talks today of the possibility of becoming involved in American politics.

Lavelle believes that his pitching abilities were a gift from God. He doesn't think that God wins ball games for him, but suggests, like many of his Blue Jay teammates, that "I think it made me better because I was able to relax and say, 'Yeah, I'm going to go out and work harder and harder.' I also think it made me a better person."

But he also is convinced that responsibility comes with faith. When God gives talent, the recipient should use it to bring honour to the Giver.

"I think that God gives us the talent, and we're to

use it. Some guys use it and some guys waste it. I always hoped that I would use it to his glory and praise, and I've always tried to strive to be the best I can and do the best I can for the Lord. Maybe, because of that attitude, I'm a better ballplayer."

While suggesting that his faith may have made him a better professional athlete, he also admits that being a born-again Christian may subject a ballplayer to additional pressures. "You're dealing more with the public than most people do. You're dealing more with the media in general, which is, in my estimation, very anti-Christian in a sense."

He's candid in his opinion of the news media: "I have a really tough time dealing with the liberal media, because I don't believe in their philosophies and I don't believe in their approach toward getting the news out."

Lavelle admits what others have suspected – that it was a difficult transition coming to the Toronto club. Suddenly he was with a new team in a new league, living in a new city and playing in a new country. "I'd known only one organization. I knew everything about them inside out. I was well-known there, and I was set up living in the San Francisco Bay area. We had a home, and our family was happy there.

"I think when you make a move such as this, everything changes. Sometimes you have to gather up your belongings and move along, and I think it's a big adjustment, especially when you're married and have children. And in a career move after so many years, it becomes difficult."

So does he regret his move to the American League, to Toronto and the Blue Jays? Not at all – despite his season-long struggles with a sore elbow (even though he never had to hit in his new league) and all of the problems that arose from that. He sees his move as a positive growing experience. "I think it's something that's worked out for the best. It's been good for me to get another perspective on things. I think it gets us out of our complacency."

The move to Toronto became easier for Gary once friendship began to grow between him and the other believers on the team. Gary says that the number of born-again Christians on the Blue Jays is a sign of what he calls a revival: "This club definitely has a lot of believers. Give credit to the fine chapel program that's in baseball and in the minor leagues now. I believe that God is starting a revival in professional sports as well as in various countries."

He becomes biblical in his observations: "The Lord is pouring our His Spirit upon all flesh. I'm really enthusiastic about what's happening in baseball and around the world."

No one can doubt Gary's enthusiasm. And although he says his eventual career goal, after baseball, is business-oriented (perhaps following some additional education), it isn't hard to imagine Gary Lavelle with a Bible in his hand and a pulpit in front of him – or with a Bible in his hand and sharing the Word of God in a locker room full of athletes.

He certainly is well-versed in the Scriptures and schedules time each day to read the Bible and pray. This, he says, is essential to spiritual growth.

"My key is definitely the time I spend in the Word and alone with God in prayer. I think that's vitally important, and sometimes I think we get involved in such hectic schedules that we start to be pulled away from doing it, and then you really feel it in your life. There's something missing there, and I know I need to have that. I need to have that time alone with God in order to get everything else right."

Although he admittedly struggled through the first weeks of life as a Blue Jay, Gary soon found himself included in the friendship among the born-again Christians, a friendship more remarkable because it cuts through racial barriers.

Lavelle says, "It's been a tremendous fellowship as far as I'm concerned. The players have such good rapport with one another here. There's good chemistry here. There are some really strong believers, and I've found that it's been very uplifting and edifying for me to be here."

He acknowledges that being a Christian changes the way blacks and whites relate to one another: "God changes people's hearts and their lives. He doesn't look on us differently if we're black or white, red or yellow. It's a matter of how a person's heart responds to Him. I think once you realize that and come together in fellowship, we put aside our colours and cultural differences and say, 'we're here to worship the same Lord.'

"I think there's a bond that takes place there. I know that I can go to the black brothers on this team and pray with them for some needs as readily as they can come to me. And I think that's what God meant for the whole world. I think that if we could all come together under the Lord Jesus Christ, it would be a much better world to live in."

Chapter 12

Ron Shepherd

There probably isn't a student in the land who hasn't been charged, at some time or another, with the most odious of offenses: unrealized potential. Many of us know the look of deep disappointment that comes to the face of a parent or teacher when telling us that with the abilities we have, we should be doing better.

Sometimes they're right; but sometimes, potential or no potential, things just don't come together.

Ron Shepherd, playing most of this season so far with the Syracuse Chiefs, would understand all about unrealized potential. The 25-year-old outfielder was drafted high by the Blue Jays – their second pick, 29th overall – in the 1979 Free Agent Draft. Everyone, including Shep, had big hopes for this bright young ballplayer. He had moved quickly through the minor league ranks, arriving in Triple A ball after his fourth year as a professional.

Yet he hasn't been able to crack the Toronto ball club to gain a permanent job; nor has he successfully cracked the mystery of major league pitching. And near the end of spring training 1986, he was demoted from the Blue Jays' 40-man roster and assigned outright to the Triple A, Syracuse club.

That doesn't mean that he's reached the end of the line – just ask Mark Eichhorn or Rick Leach. But it was a severe blow to the career of a man who's known by his teammates as one of the most likable men ever to share the Blue Jays bench.

His return to Syracuse was especially tough to take for Ron, because he came off a fine performance during a partial season in Triple A in 1985. Playing with that club in the middle of the season, his batting averaged .308 in 37 games. He'd begun the year on the disabled list, with tendonitis in his right elbow. When he was reactivated, he spent the first part of the campaign with the Blue Jays, but a low batting average bought him his ticket to Syracuse.

But Ron's excellent performance in Triple A earned him a second chance with the Jays in '85 – however, he still couldn't solve the riddle of batting in the big leagues. His major league average last season is almost 200 points below his minor league mark – just .114 in 35 at-bats. He also spent time with the Jays in 1984, and his overall major league batting average is an even more sombre .103. Many of his appearances were as a pinch runner or occasioned by late-inning defensive moves.

Even if he'd been hitting well, Ron would have the unenviable task of trying to break into an outfield now populated by his talented friends Jesse Barfield, Lloyd Moseby, and George Bell.

Jerry Haworth has watched Shep play almost every big league inning in which the tall Texan has appeared. He thinks he could still make it in the majors – but perhaps not with the Blue Jays.

Haworth says, "Ronnie Shepherd's a good young man who's learned a lot about himself in the last few years. He's had to face some adversity – first of all not getting to the big league level as fast as he'd hoped, and then when he got here he couldn't play very much because there were good people in front of him.

front of him.

"Maybe if he gets a little more of an opportunity, maybe even with another ball club, he might blossom as Mitch Webster did, who's done really well with Montreal. Ronnie just has to continue to be patient."

The broadcaster's expert eye has seen some of that unrealized potential in Shepherd: "He reminds me of a young George Foster. When I grew up in San Francisco, Foster was a tall, gangly kid who struck out and looked terrible. The Giants let him go – they traded him to Cincinnati for Frank Duffy, and as they say, the rest is history. Foster was part of the Big Red Machine.

"Ronnie could be in that category, but he just has to play every day. He got cast with a great ball club, a great organization. They'll stick up for him."

Haworth suggests that Shepherd has his priorities in the right place to handle the kind of disappointments he's encountered: "Ronnie's been able to handle it pretty well. I think now that the apple of his eye is his son Jeremiah. He can handle his profession now because he's got a great wife (Janda) and child and puts everything into perspective well."

Ron Shepherd might have good reason to be frustrated or angry. A promising career has taken a sudden down-turn, and he might have taken it out on himself or on the club. He does neither.

About the Blue Jays, he says, "I think they've been fair. There are some people here who've been really nice and very honest with me, and I like that."

And regarding his future, he's retained his confidence: "The only thing I anticipate is being on the major league level. As to where that is, I don't know right now. More than likely it will probably be here, but I anticipate being in the major leagues somewhere."

His confidence isn't cocky or arrogant; instead, Shep shows a peaceful kind of contentment and assurance that everything will be all right. Like his close friend Jesse Barfield, Ron is a born-again Christian. His favourite Bible verse is: "I can do all things through Christ, who strengthens me" (Philippians 4:13).

When he quotes that statement, he's not talking only – or even primarily – about baseball. Ron Shepherd is a man who's learned to deal with life as a whole, and despite setbacks in his career, he does so with great success.

He says that his life turned full circle when he encountered Christ, through the influence of Barfield.

But it wasn't only Jesse's influence – Ron had an experience where he encountered Jesus face to face, in a dream. Here's his story:

"I think the Lord had a lot to do with my life even when I didn't know about it. It started out with a couple of dreams, in which I believe the Lord was talking to me.

"There were some things that were going on in my life, a lot of sexual things. I was never into drugs, but I got into a lot of sexual activities. It was relatively easy. As a ballplayer you get to do just about anything you want, and I thought that was cool: go with everybody else, go get the girls and do whatever.

"But I'd been hurt emotionally by a couple of girls and I was pretty well tired of them. And then I had this dream. You know how guys always picture the most beautiful girl they can imagine? Well, I saw her. She was standing about ten feet from me, and there was a force between us. She was pulling me toward her. Remember, at that time I'd become sort of an introvert – I didn't want anything to do with women, because they'd hurt me.

"But in the dream, the girl was pulling me toward her, the most beautiful girl a guy could picture in his mind! I was saying, 'No, I don't want anything to do with this.' I was trying to push her back, but it was still drawing me. And the closer I got, the uglier it got. I don't just mean physically ugly – there was a real spiritual ugliness there, something that just grabs you and twists you.

"Eventually, I got to about three feet from this incredibly ugly thing. I was crying, and there was nothing I could do. Finally, I just dropped my hands and said, 'God help me.'

"Then, everything kind of eased up. And a really bright light shone from somehwere behind me. Whatever this thing was in front of me, it just took off and shot away.

"I turned around, and as I turned I saw what appeared to me to be Jesus. He just held his arms out, and I grabbed Him. I felt that I had no physical weight at all. I couldn't describe what He looked like, but later my wife's aunt, who's a born-again Christian, showed me the description of Christ in the book of Revelation, and it was exactly who I had seen in the dream."

Perhaps surprisingly, Ron didn't follow up the astounding experience he'd had through his dream – at least , not immediately. But he knew that God had shown him important truths about the destructiveness of sin, and the answer: Jesus Christ. But he also knew that accepting that answer was going to mean a major overhaul of Ron Shepherd.

Six months later, during spring training 1983,

Ron encountered phase two of God's plan to draw him into the love of Christ. This time it was no dream – it came through a very real, muscular, hard-hitting right fielder named Jesse Barfield.

Jesse and Ron had been close companions, but Ron knew that Jesse had become a born-again Christian, and he was frankly a little afraid of his friend at the time. He tells the story this way:

"At that time I was heavily into profanity. I thought it was the 'in' thing to do, to swear and curse.

"I was running in the outfield one day and Jesse said, 'Shep, how're you doing?'

" 'Not a [expletive deleted] thing,' I said, and I started swearing – and then it kind of hit me: 'Oh man, I forgot. He's one of those Jesus freaks now.' And I kind of dodged him for the rest of the day, because I was pretty embarrassed about it.

"That night or the next, I was sitting in my room at the Ramada Inn, and I heard a knock on the door. In came Jesse and Marla and their little boy. And they had a couple of Bibles stacked on the stroller as they rolled in."

That was it. God had pursued Ron Shepherd far enough; the young outfielder surrendered his life to Christ that night, praying with his friends. He's gone on to become one of the most dedicated Christians ever to wear a Blue Jays uniform.

He doesn't understand all of the career ups and downs that he's experienced, including those of this season, but he believes that God will see him through them. He says, "My faith in the Lord and what He'll do for me and my family is incredible right now" – and he means it.

God will always be first in Ron's list of priorities. He remembers one occasion when he was tempted to lay his Bible aside, because some of his teammates thought his "religion" was hurting his concentration, and thus his performance.

"I was hitting the ball, but I wasn't getting any hits. My average was way down compared to the year before. I couldn't figure out what was going on. But at the time, that's when I was really digging into the Word, searching for the Lord. And people would say to me, 'Well, Shep, maybe you should put your Bible aside and get out and mingle with the guys a little more. Go have a drink.' All worldly things.

"And the Lord just kind of slapped me 'up side the head,' to tell you the truth. He said, 'Watch out – remember, these same things happened to Job.'

"And man, that just hit me like a ton of bricks. I started laughing. I'll never forget that day and that joyous feeling. And every day someone would come up and tell me to put my Bible aside or to forget about the Lord. That's when I dug deeper into it.

"You know, it didn't improve my hitting any. But I worked harder, and I knew that the Lord would get me out of it. And sure enough, the same winter I led the winter league in home runs, and I was second in RBI's, stolen bases and runs scored.

"The Lord let me know that if I'd hold on to Him, He'd show me the way and show me the right things to do."

Shepherd is determined to do what's right before God. For example, he, along with several other players on the Jays, had agreed to meet with a group of 200 men from several churches after a Blue Jays game last summer.

The game must have set a record for rain delay. When the downpour struck, the Jays were ahead; when the game resumed some three hours later, the Blue Jays quickly fell behind and lost the match.

The dressing room was as unhappy a place as you could find that afternoon.

As the players changed and got ready to go home after a long and frustrating day's work, 200 men and boys waited on the busses, not sure that they would still be able to meet their heroes, but reluctant to miss the opportunity. As the Jays emerged from the clubhouse, some simply (and understandably) didn't feel up to meeting a group of strangers. The meeting had been planned in advance, but the afternoon's activities had completely destroyed both schedule and good spirits.

The organizer was quite worried that no oe would be willing to show up, and David Fisher, who'd helped set it up, later confessed he thought the whole thing had washed out. But then Ron Shepherd and Lloyd Moseby came through the door. They grabbed Tony Fernandez and marched down the block to the busses, where they climbed on and shared their faith in Jesus with a couple of hundred awestruck fans.

When Ron Shepherd – or Lloyd, or Tony – makes a commitment, you can count on it!

Perhaps it would be easy to have faith in God if you were at the top of the league in hitting or pitching, although those situations present a different set of temptations. But the faith of a guy like Ron Shepherd, who's struggling to make it in the game he loves, offers a true revelation of what Christianity can do in the inner person.

Ron would much rather be playing in front of the 30,000 or 40,000 fans who turn out for Blue Jays home games, instead of the relative handful that watch the Chiefs in Syracuse. He jokes about the lack of media attention, claiming that being ignored by the media "gives me more time to think about what I have to do."

He believes that he'll be at home in some major league ball park, some day. But until then, the six-foot-four Texan is content to leave his life in the hands of his God. He figures that God does a better job as manager than he does anyway.

Chapter 13

David Fisher

Batting practice is over, and the Toronto Blue Jays have returned to their clubhouse, where they're making final preparations for their Sunday afternoon game. Willie Upshaw is probably trying to get his glove back from Lloyd Moseby; Tony Fernandez is doing a little last-minute work with a small one-hand weight; Mark Eichhorn, who's slightly mad, might be break-dancing.

A tall, red-haired man in metal-framed glasses quietly enters the locker room, and Moseby quickly takes charge, announcing that the chapel service will start in five minutes in the weight room.

Anywhere from six to fifteen of the team wander in that direction and sit on the floor or a piece of equipment. The service is brief – there's prayer and someone, perhaps the tall man himself, opens the Bible and shares a message that's appropriate for the day and for the men who've gathered in the room. There may be some discussion of the message or a time for sharing from their life situations.

There's a genuine sense of sharing and companionship among these men who've taken twenty minutes of pre-game preparation time to pray and study the Bible. They do it every week, before every Sunday game.

The red-haired chaplain, David Fisher, has also spent time with most of the players that day. He often takes them a Christian book, and before chapel he's walked around the lockers, smiling and speaking briefly with his friends.

When the service is over, the Blue Jay players head back to the benches in front of their lockers to pull on the last pieces of equipment, to talk to their teammates, or just to sit quietly, getting ready to play major league baseball. Fisher slips out of the dressing room and into the visiting team's locker room, where he finds the chapel leader from that squad. The same procedure follows, and a service is held with the visiting players.

David has been doing this ever since the Blue Jays began playing ball as Toronto's entry to the American League. In fact, he was doing it even before that, working with Montreal Expos' chapel.

He continues as chapel coordinator for both teams, traveling to Toronto or Montreal each week from his home in Peterborough, Ontario. On a week when both teams have home games, he'll arrange for someone to coordinate the service in one city while he visits the other. He also frequently visits the Syracuse Chiefs and has conducted chapels for basketball teams and at golf tournaments.

For Fisher, it's a labour of love. He does all of this work entirely on a volunteer basis; he receives no pay for his dedicated service. When he has travel expenses – such as a trip to a Baseball Chapels meeting in Tampa, Florida, this spring – he has to come up with the money himself.

He also runs an outreach known as Epistle Sports Ministries, through which he maintains communication by letter with athletes in a number of sports. David writes to them especially at times when they're under added pressure, such as when they're traded, injured, or demoted to the minor leagues.

He also places Bibles and Christian literature in the baseball team clubhouses.

In fact, that's how he became involved in ministry to athletes in the first place. Unlike the spokesmen for many ministries involving athletes, David has never played any professional sport – although he's almost fanatical about the slow-pitch team he's involved with. He plays an intense first base on the squad.

David was earlier involved with the Gideons, a group of Christian businessmen who provide Bibles to a wide variety of places, from motels to schools. He says that his interest in the Gideons, in combination with his operation of a Bible bookstore, produced in him a growing "commitment to distribute God's word, to get out the Good News." I love what the Gideons do, but sometimes I wanted to give Bibles to people whom the Gideons aren't set up to give Bibles to – such as ballplayers."

He had a special desire to present the Word of God to the Montreal Expos. He says, "I've loved the Expos ever since they came into existence. I just felt led of the Lord, back in 1976, to present a Bible to every one of the Expos.

That was his goal, but he really didn't know how to go about it. Fisher knew of the organization known as Bible Chapel, and he contacted them for advice. He was told to get in touch with Gary Carter, the all-star catcher who was then the Expos' chapel leader.

David recalls that he wrote to Carter, "and he thought it was a good idea. He lined up our first meeting in May 1976, and I went down there for a Sunday with 35 Bibles, one for every player on the roster, all the coaches, the manager, general manager and the trainer."

On the way to Montreal, Fisher couldn't remember quite how he'd gotten himself into that situation. He was nervous – "I'd never even talked to a baseball player before."

He remembers that he felt like a kid, but was determined not to allow the thrill of the occasion to get in the way of the purpose that was sending him to the Olympic Stadium. "The real reason was to give out the Word of God."

Since that day, David Fisher has met almost every player in the National and American Leagues, as well as stars from other sports. He continues in his resolve to keep his own desires as a fan out of the way. He's never asked a player for a souvenir, although Montreal's Andre Dawson offered Fisher a bat and since then has given his chaplain friend dozens of bats from other stars.

It wasn't long after the presentation of those Bibles that David became more intimately involved in the chapel program in Montreal. He was an unofficial volunteer for several years and was invited in 1980 to become a member of the staff of Baseball Chapel.

His experience with the Expos encouraged Fisher to get in on the ground floor with the Blue Jays. Watson Spoelstra, then the head of Baseball Chapel, asked him if he would arrange for speakers for Blue Jays chapel, and he asked David himself to speak on one of the early Sundays.

On the first Sunday home game for the franchise, Fisher showed up laden with Bibles for the new Jays, each one with the Blue Jays logo engraved in gold on the cover. He's been involved with the Blue Jays chapel program ever since.

On some Sundays David doesn't even get to see the game. But as often as he can, he's in the stands watching his boys.

His cheering pattern is discernibly different from that of the fans around him. They cheer for the Blue Jays. David cheers for his friends from chapel on either squad, and he prays.

He says, "I watch them with pride, and I pray. It's a completely different experience, and I love it. I pray for the guys who are believers on the visiting teams too."

And what happens when two believers face each other, pitcher against hitter? What if Jesse Barfield is hitting against a Christian who just sat in chapel with David Fisher?

Fisher smiles. "I have mixed feelings. I don't know what I want to happen. I guess, being a home team guy, I'd like to see Jesse hit it out of the park."

This season, the Blue Jays chapel has augmented its program. The teams still meet for Sunday chapel services, as they have since 1977, but David has promoted some additional Bible studies for the weeks when the Jays are at home. Often the studies are led by former pro athletes Paul Henderson (of hockey fame) or Gord Barwell, once a wide receiver with the Saskatchewan entry in the Canadian Football League.

Fisher is unselfish about leadership in the chapel program; he's delighted to involve other people who can minister effectively to the athletes. But he admits that it's sometimes hard to find people who'll simply care about the players because they're people, not because they're heroes of the Toronto Blue Jays.

That's the key to his success – Fisher has never come in as a grown-up groupie. He's always talking with friends as a friend. He's quiet and not at all pushy, but he's done a great deal for the men who play baseball in Toronto.

His approach is also important. Many sports ministries use players to reach out to fans with the Gospel, but Fisher is concerned essentially with reaching out to the players. There isn't a whiff of exploitation in his work. His concern is with the ballplayers, not with using the ballplayers as celebrity spokesmen for a ministry.

Blue Jays past and present have nothing but praise for the tall, red-haired man who's given so much time and energy to them. Gary Lavelle credits baseball chapel with being the catalyst to bring a real moving of God among the ballplayers. Steve Davis says that he needs the chapel services to grow in his Christian life. Lloyd Moseby, Tony Fernandez, Willie Upshaw and the other Jays say something that may be even more significant: David Fisher is their friend.

They appreciate him, and they know how much he does for them. But if they ever tried to thank him, David would simply say, "Give the glory to God."

Chapter 14

How You Can Join The Jays

I have dedicated this book to Luke and Aaron Knowles, my two young sons. There's very little likelihood that either of them will ever play for the Toronto Blue Jays. They'll probably never pitch like Mark Eichhorn, hit like Jesse Barfield, or field like Tony Fernandez.

But I hope that they'll follow these players, and the other eight whose stories you've read, in the most important area of life – in knowing God.

When the Toronto Blue Jays take to the field, they need the numbers on their backs so the fans can tell them apart. In their sharp, blue on white uniforms, they look very much alike. We need to see number 15 to know it's Lloyd Moseby, or number 17 so we can be sure we're right when we cheer Kelly Gruber.

But off the field, these men are very unlike one another. As Steve Davis discovered, they're as different, one from the other, as any other human beings. Lloyd Moseby is a walking field of positive vibrations. Mark Eichhorn is just a bit crazy. Tony Fernandez is often very serious. Jeff Hearron is determined. Jesse Barfield is self-confident. Willie Upshaw is shy. Ron Shepherd is mellow and peaceful. Kelly Gruber is intense.

Their experiences are different from one another. They all play ball awfully well, but their paths to the Blue Jays uniform are diverse. Gary Lavelle came to the team as a seasoned pro. Don Gordon, who took Gary's place in the bullpen, is a brand-new rookie. Willie Upshaw made the team and never looked back. Mark Eichhorn had his chance, failed, and made a miraculous recovery this season. Ron Shepherd is still looking for the miracle.

Some of them are married – Lavelle for over a decade, Steve Davis for only a few years. Some are parents. Some are bachelors – Hearron, Gruber and Eichhorn – with a wholly different set of problems and questions.

While all of these players have close friends on the team, none of them is a "best buddy" with all of the others.

They come from different backgrounds, ranging from Gary Lavelle's birthplace of Scranton, Pennsylvania, to Tony Fernandez' home in San Pedro de Macoris, in the Dominican Republic. Some came from poor families, others from middle class homes. Some dropped out of school to play ball; others came via university teams. Five are black; six are white. If they didn't play baseball for the same squad, they'd have only one thing in common.

But all would agree that one thing is the most important in the world to them: their faith in God and their relationship with Jesus Christ.

To a man, they insist that the true answers to the problems and questions of life are found in the Word of God, the Bible. If they could sit down individually with each of the readers of this book, they would do two things: they'd tell you what a difference Christ has made in their lives, and they'd open their well-used Bibles and show you how you can find the same life-changing answers that they've discovered.

Willie Upshaw, the quiet man, might open his Bible to one of his favourite verses and read:

"For all have sinned and come short of the glory of God" (Romans 3:23). That verse, written by the Apostle Paul, states clearly and simply the trap in which each of us finds himself. God has expectations for his creations; He made us to live holy lives, in loving relationship with Him.

But we've rebelled – that's what sin is, rebellion and disobedience against God – and we now fall far short of His requirements. We're doomed to live this life, and eternity, apart from Him. Eternity away from God is called "hell". Willie's verse tells us, simply, that we're all in the same terrible situation.

But Lloyd Moseby would sit next to his friend Willie, turn back to the book of Isaiah in the Old Testament, and read his favourite verses:

"He is despised and rejected of men, a man of sorrows, and acquainted with grief, and we hid as it were our faces from Him; He was despised and we esteemed Him not. Surely He hath borne our griefs, and carried our sorrows . . . But He was wounded for our transgressions, He was bruised for our iniquities; the chastisement for our peace was upon Him, and with His stripes we are healed. All we like sheep have gone astray; we have turned every one to his own way, and the Lord hath laid on Him the iniquity of us all" (Isaiah 53:3-6).

These verses show us the same truth as Romans 3:23 – we're sinners. That's what "transgressions" and "iniquities" mean – sin! But there's a remarkable story in Lloyd's favourite passage – the story of someone who carried the penalty for your sins, someone who was wounded for your rebellion.

That someone is Jesus Christ. He is God's Son, and because He is God, He was able to carry the punishment for the sin of us all! That means that the penalty for sin has been paid, and you need no longer fall short of God's glory. You can be carried back into His presence, now and for eternity, by Jesus!

We've all gone astray, but like these men on the Blue Jays, you can come back to the loving relationship God intended for us. To do so, you must accept the fact that you've sinned, then turn from that rebellion and ask Jesus to be your rescuer – your Saviour.

He's eager to do that. That's what's meant in Don Gordon's favourite verse: Jesus said, "Come unto Me, all ye that labour and are heavy laden, and I will give you rest" (Matthew 11:28). Perhaps as you've read the stories of these ballplayers, you've identified with their situations – the void that Lloyd Moseby talked about or the struggles within himself that Steve Davis referred to. Perhaps you even know the feeling of guilt that Ron Shepherd alluded to in his story. Or maybe, like Tony Fernandez, you've wandered away from the truth you knew in former years.

Jesus says, "Come unto Me." All those burdens and problems can be taken care of. You don't have to carry them any longer.

Kelly Gruber pointed to this verse: "This one thing I do, forgetting those things which are behind, and reaching forth unto those things which are before, I press toward the mark for the prize of the high calling of God in Jesus Christ" (Philippians 3:13, 14). Almost every person knows the feeling of wanting to forget the messes and the mistakes we've made in our lives. This verse says it's possible – but you can't do it in your own strength.

Ron Shepherd shared this verse with us: "I can do all things through Christ, who strengthens me" (Philippians 4:13). That's the secret of leaving your past behind and walking on in a new life. And that's what being "born again" means – allowing Jesus Christ to wipe out the failures in your past, and beginning again in the strength that's yours in Christ, when you make Him Lord – the boss – of your life!

Gary Lavelle referred to this verse from the book of Acts: "And it shall come to pass in the last days, saith God, I will pour out of My Spirit upon all flesh" (Acts 2:17). When you commit your life to Christ, God begins a loving, intimate relationship with you. In fact, He places his Holy Spirit in your heart, to give you strength and power and guidance to live the kind of life you want to live, the kind of life that these men on the Blue Jays have discovered – a life of joy, peace and even fun, as Jeff Hearron described.

This relationship with Christ, of which you've read page after page from the life stories of these eleven men, can be yours. You can be set free from the bondage of sin, free to be the person God made you to be. You need to turn from rebellion against God, confess your sin to Him, and ask Jesus to be your Saviour and Lord.

The benefits are astounding!

Jesse Barfield pointed to some of them: "Greater is He that is in you than He that is in the world" (I John 4:4). That's a promise of victory over sin and over the influence of evil. That's the key to peace and happiness in a sinful world – having the One who's greater, the Holy Spirit of God, living in you as is promised in the verse referred to by Gary Lavelle.

165

And Tony Fernandez chose one of the greatest promises in the entire Bible: "All things work together for good to them that love God" (Romans 8:28). Too often, only the first part of this statement is quoted – but we know that all things don't always work together for good, for everyone. This is a promise from God to His children, a promise which states that whatever we face – demotion for Ron Shepherd, temptation for Kelly Gruber or injury to Gary Lavelle – God will bring good for them and you out of the situation.

If you love Him.

I encourage you to follow the example of these great ballplayers who are also fine men of God. Each of them has surrendered his life to Jesus Christ, and each says that life just keeps getting better and better, as each of them learns to walk with God.

You can know that same joy. Simply accept the truths from the Bible that they've shared with you, and ask God to take control of your life. That's how you can join these particular Jays.

If you would like more information on how you can know Jesus Christ personally, please contact; Crossroads Christian Communications Inc. at 100 Huntley St., Toronto, Ont. Canada M4Y 2L1.